SUPPORT AND RETAIN EDUCATORS OF COLOR

SUPPORT AND RETAIN EDUCATORS OF COLOR

6 PRINCIPLES FOR CULTURALLY AFFIRMING LEADERSHIP

ANDREA TERRERO **GABBADON**

Arlington, Virginia USA

2800 Shirlington Road, Suite 1001 • Arlington, VA 22206 USA
Phone: 800-933-2723 or 703-578-9600 • Fax: 703-575-5400
Website: www.ascd.org • Email: member@ascd.org
Author guidelines: www.ascd.org/write

Penny Reinart, *Deputy Executive Director;* Genny Ostertag, *Managing Director, Book Acquisitions & Editing;* Susan Hills, *Senior Acquisitions Editor;* Mary Beth Nielsen, *Director, Book Editing;* Jennifer L. Morgan, *Editor;* Thomas Lytle, *Creative Director;* Donald Ely, *Art Director;* Marzia Motta/The Hatcher Group, *Graphic Designer;* Valerie Younkin, *Senior Production Designer;* Circle Graphics, *Typesetter;* Kelly Marshall, *Production Manager;* Shajuan Martin, *E-Publishing Specialist*

Copyright © 2023 Andrea Terrero Gabbadon. All rights reserved. It is illegal to reproduce copies of this work in print or electronic format (including reproductions displayed on a secure intranet or stored in a retrieval system or other electronic storage device from which copies can be made or displayed) without the prior written permission of the publisher. By purchasing only authorized electronic or print editions and not participating in or encouraging piracy of copyrighted materials, you support the rights of authors and publishers. Readers who wish to reproduce or republish excerpts of this work in print or electronic format may do so for a small fee by contacting the Copyright Clearance Center (CCC), 222 Rosewood Dr., Danvers, MA 01923, USA (phone: 978-750-8400; fax: 978-646-8600; web: www.copyright.com). To inquire about site licensing options or any other reuse, contact ASCD Permissions at www.ascd.org/permissions or permission@ascd.org. For a list of vendors authorized to license ASCD e-books to institutions, see www.ascd.org/epubs. Send translation inquiries to translations@ascd.org.

ASCD® is a registered trademark of Association for Supervision and Curriculum Development. All other trademarks contained in this book are the property of, and reserved by, their respective owners, and are used for editorial and informational purposes only. No such use should be construed to imply sponsorship or endorsement of the book by the respective owners.

All web links in this book are correct as of the publication date below but may have become inactive or otherwise modified since that time. If you notice a deactivated or changed link, please email books@ascd.org with the words "Link Update" in the subject line. In your message, please specify the web link, the book title, and the page number on which the link appears.

PAPERBACK ISBN: 978-1-4166-3212-2   ASCD product #123018   n7/23
PDF EBOOK ISBN: 978-1-4166-3213-9; see Books in Print for other formats.
Quantity discounts are available: email programteam@ascd.org or call 800-933-2723, ext. 5773, or 703-575-5773. For desk copies, go to www.ascd.org/deskcopy.

Library of Congress Cataloging-in-Publication Data

Names: Gabbadon, Andrea Terrero, author.
Title: Support and retain educators of color : 6 principles for culturally affirming leadership / Andrea Terrero Gabbadon.
Description: Arlington, Virginia : ASCD, 2023. | Includes bibliographical references and index.
Identifiers: LCCN 2023009782 (print) | LCCN 2023009783 (ebook) | ISBN 9781416632122 (paperback) | ISBN 9781416632139 (pdf)
Subjects: LCSH: Minority teachers—Recruiting—United States. | Teacher turnover—Prevention—United States. | School environment—United States.
Classification: LCC LB2835.25 .G34 2023 (print) | LCC LB2835.25 (ebook) | DDC 371.10089—dc23/eng/20230313
LC record available at https://lccn.loc.gov/2023009782
LC ebook record available at https://lccn.loc.gov/2023009783

---

32 31 30 29 28 27 26 25 24 23   1 2 3 4 5 6 7 8 9 10 11 12

SUPPORT AND RETAIN EDUCATORS OF COLOR

6 PRINCIPLES FOR CULTURALLY AFFIRMING LEADERSHIP

Preface _____ vii

Introduction _____ 1

1 | PRINCIPLE 1: Acknowledge That Educator Diversity Matters _____ 5

2 | PRINCIPLE 2: Cultivate Reflection and Self-Awareness _____ 18

3 | PRINCIPLE 3: Assess and Plan for Action _____ 42

4 | PRINCIPLE 4: Commit to Sustainable and High-Impact Instructional Supports _____ 69

5 | PRINCIPLE 5: Foster Supportive Environments for Culturally Responsive Approaches _____ 86

6 | PRINCIPLE 6: Lead for an Inclusive Community _____ 110

Appendix A: Social Identity Reflection Tool _____ 141

Appendix B: Guiding Principles for Effective Pulse Meetings _____ 143

Appendix C: Sample Topics and Questions for Pulse Meetings _____ 145

Appendix D: Pulse Meeting Agenda _____ 148

References _____ 149

Index _____ 164

About the Author _____ 170

Preface

It is critical to use clear and precise language to discuss ethnic-racial identity, racism, and other important topics. The language we use is important, particularly considering the historical context of how race and racial categories were constructed on false and manufactured pseudoscience (Cohen, 2016), weaponized to legitimate oppression and inequality (Omi & Winant, 1988), and sanitized for the purpose of erasing the legacy of racism (Pollock, 2004). The language we use held power then and holds power now. At the same time, language (and our understanding of these constructs) is dynamic and has changed over time in response to civil rights movements, community organizing, and struggles for equity. Following is context for some of the language choices related to ethnicity, race, and related constructs I made while writing this book.

Support and Retain Educators of Color focuses on a specific demographic of the U.S. educator workforce: individuals who represent the global majority, yet are referred to as "racial minorities" in an attempt to maintain the normativity of the white majority and contribute to the marginalization of non-Eurocentric ways of being, forms of knowledge, languages, and cultures. Although other terms exist, such as Black, Indigenous, and People of Color (BIPOC) and People of the Global Majority (POGM), among others, I use "people of color" to describe a wide range of groups, including Latino/x, African American or Black, Asian American and Pacific Islander, Native

American and tribal communities, North African and Middle Eastern, and other people groups that have been racialized as "nonwhite." I use the term "people of color" or "educators of color," imbued with both merits and constraints, to be consistent with other scholarship about educator diversity. For more on this topic, see Rita Kohli (2021) or Conra Gist and Travis Bristol (2022), who have been some of my teachers from afar and have inspired my thinking and research.

You will notice that I vary the terminology I use in this book. It is my intention to use the preferred racial categories and terms communicated by specific ethnic-racial groups to describe themselves. At times, however, I choose to use language that is consistent with racial labels in a particular data source or reference. For example, I use the term "Hispanic" in an analysis of National Center for Education Statistics data, following the practice of the creators of that source. When not referring explicitly to these data sets, I use the term "Latino/x," a neologism that blends "Latino" (a pan-ethnic term to describe peoples of Latin American origin) and the inclusive, gender-neutral "Latinx." Both these terms fall short of conveying the rich cultural, ethnic, linguistic, racial, and ancestral diversity of Latin America but are commonly used to describe the peoples who have been placed in this racial category—while still being subject to critique (Noe-Bustamente et al., 2020).

At its core, "the language we use to categorize one another racially is imperfect" (Tatum, 2017, p. 97), as the social construct of race was created—and maintained—for nefarious and exploitative purposes. Although imperfect, language remains a tool that we can use to bring awareness to the permanence of race and racism in order to create change.

Introduction

Dear Instructional Leader,

 First, a warm "Congratulations!" If you are holding this book, it is likely that you have already thought deeply about the importance of ethnic-racial diversity in your school context and desire to make strides toward retaining educators of color. The fact that you have invested in this book also signals your personal and professional commitment to fostering an antiracist organizational context in which educators of color thrive.

 I wrote this book as a blueprint to support instructional leaders and teams—including principals, assistant principals, instructional coaches, and grade and content leaders—in their efforts to support and retain educators of color in their schools and districts. Educators of color remain vastly underrepresented in teaching. Approximately 20 percent of the teacher workforce identifies as a person of color, whereas over 50 percent of the student population are students of color. In contrast, nearly 80 percent of teachers identify as white, and the majority identify as white women (National Center for Education Statistics [NCES], 2020b). Altogether, the overwhelming ethnic-racial, cultural, and linguistic mismatch between students and the educator workforce holds significant implications for students' academic and educational experiences. Some of these implications will be discussed in more depth in forthcoming chapters. Educators of color are likewise underrepresented in positions of leadership and administration (NCES, 2020a), resulting in ethnic-racial and cultural gaps between school leaders and the students and staff they serve.

Research indicates the presence of educators of color in schools is associated with many benefits for all students—and students of color in particular. Yet turnover is higher for educators of color than for white educators. Studies indicate educators of color often experience organizational conditions that are not affirming or inclusive of their identities and backgrounds (Pizarro & Kohli, 2020; Stanley, 2022). Such turnover is costly, not only bearing significant economic implications for schools (Watlington et al., 2010) but also eliminating opportunities for all students to have educators of color leading schools and classrooms. With these facts in mind, this book equips instructional leaders (professionals whose responsibilities are anchored in recruiting, hiring, supporting, and retaining educators) and instructional leadership teams with concrete culturally affirming strategies to help educators of color feel valued and seen, thus enhancing their desire to stay in their schools and the profession.

Culturally affirming is a term that will emerge quite often in the forthcoming pages. Guided by years of extensive scholarship, many interviews with educators of color across the continental United States, and my own experiences as a teacher and instructional leader in traditional public and charter schools, I define culturally affirming leadership practices as those *characterized by supportive and positive relationships across lines of difference.* Such relationships are cross-cultural, interracial, intergenerational, and emblematic of sincere connection and belonging. Grounded in antiracism, these practices lend themselves to culturally affirming systems and schools in which there is robust representation of diverse educators, not just as classroom leaders but also in positions of power and leadership.

Culturally affirming organizations diverge from Eurocentric, standardized approaches to professionalism, teaching, and learning and acknowledge, value, and authentically reflect diverse backgrounds and cultural ways of knowing in every aspect of the school. Leaders who engage in culturally affirming practices understand that identity is complex and holds historical, social, and political significance inside and outside of schools. They understand that markers of identity cannot be considered in isolation; rather, ethnicity, gender, language, and social status all interact with one another, which means that racism can be compounded with sexism, linguicism, classism, and other forms of oppression. These leaders understand and seek to dismantle all forms of stereotypes on the basis of social identity, prejudice, intolerance, and colorblindness in their schools. Lastly, these leaders understand that pursuit of culturally affirming schools goes hand in hand with pursuing antiracist systems, educational excellence, liberation, and healing with and for students of color and the communities they represent.

Multiple studies have explored the benefits of teacher diversity and strategies to recruit educators of color. Few resources focus on supporting and retaining them, however, and materials specifically geared toward those who hold positions as instructional leaders are absent. I have focused my attention on addressing this gap through research, interviewing educators of diverse ethnic-racial and gender backgrounds and school contexts. The contents of this book consist of best practices drawn from school leaders and scholar-activists who have piloted many of the ideas and strategies mentioned here. Their work is carefully cited in the References as well as in the Beyond the Text section at the end of each chapter, and I encourage you to explore these resources to further your learning. I look forward to adding to this book in the future with new developments and discoveries about what works in schools.

Until then, *pa'lante!* Onward!

PRINCIPLE 1:
Acknowledge That Educator Diversity Matters

In diversity there is beauty and there is strength.

—Maya Angelou

Children need role models—they need to see themselves in the faces of their educators. We need educators who can relate to the lives of diverse students, and who can connect those students to larger worlds and greater possibilities.

—Richard Riley

This book is designed to equip instructional leaders with knowledge and tools to nurture culturally affirming conditions for educators of color.* The goal of this work is straightforward: to retain a diverse educator workforce that reflects the rich ethnic-racial, linguistic, and cultural backgrounds of the students we serve.

---

* The term "of color" describes the racial categorization of non-white people groups. The National Center for Education Statistics (NCES) uses the following categories: Black, Hispanic, American Indian/Alaska Native, and two or more races. In line with recommendations from the Asian Pacific Institute on Gender-Based Violence, Asian American and Pacific Islander are referenced together (e.g., Asian American Pacific Islander or AAPI).

Educator diversity matters! This chapter makes the urgent case for educator diversification for the good of schools and society, analyzes the benefits associated with educators of color and their impact on students, and explores factors that have led to the racial imbalance between educators and students. The evidence all points to the value of the first principle of culturally affirming instructional leadership: *Acknowledge that diversity matters.*

The Case for Educator Diversity

Take a moment to reflect on the role of schools in society. History reveals that at different points in time, schools have addressed a slew of cultural and social demands.

- During the Common School era, schools were deemed "the great equalizers" (Mann, 1848) and they adopted a universal curriculum for the purpose of creating "common" (read: shared) values, norms, and methods across schools (Rury, 2012).
- During the Industrial Age, schools emphasized technical skills and workplace readiness to generate an efficient, skilled, and globally competitive workforce (Spring, 2019).
- In moments of social change (e.g., early 20th-century urbanization), schools focused on teaching students ethics and civic responsibility for the purpose of developing moral citizenry (Spring, 2019).

The demands of globalization and immigration patterns in recent decades have caused seismic cultural shifts in many communities. Schools are expected to equip students to be forward-thinking, culturally dexterous, and civically active in the global community. Boosting the number of educators of color supports these goals, as these educators can often serve as "mirrors" to reflect the backgrounds of students of color and "windows" to expand students' horizons to diverse lived experiences and perspectives.

Diversifying the educator workforce also advances democratic ideals, particularly equality of representation. However, American teachers do not currently reflect the students they serve. In 2000, children whose families identified as white made up approximately 61 percent of children enrolled in public schools (NCES, 2019a). This percentage decreased to 46 percent in

2020 (NCES, 2022). Conversely, the proportion of students of color (including Hispanic, American Indian/Alaska Native, Black, Asian, Pacific Islander, and two or more races) rose to 64 percent. Notably, the percentage of Hispanic students increased from 16 to 28 percent of student enrollment. Despite these rapidly changing student demographics, approximately 79 percent of the educator workforce self-identifies as white (NCES, 2019b). In an impassioned call to action to rectify growing ethnic-racial gaps between educators and students, former U.S. Secretary of Education Richard Riley (1998) said, "If we are to be responsive to the special demands and great opportunities of our nation's pluralistic makeup, we should develop a teaching force that is diverse, as well" (p. 19). Our collective responsibility as educators is to heed this call to action and ready our schools to attract, support, and retain educators of color.

Benefits of a Diverse Educator Workforce

A considerable amount of research reveals that educators of color are linked with positive effects on students who mirror their backgrounds. Of central importance is the potential for educators of color to positively influence opportunity gaps, or what Gloria Ladson-Billings (2006) refers to as "the education debt," for socioeconomically disadvantaged communities and children of color who have been historically, economically, and sociopolitically deprived of equal educational opportunities (see also Carter & Welner, 2013). The following characteristics of educators of color demonstrate research-backed benefits to racially and ethnically diverse students:

- They exhibit high expectations leading to increased student learning and academic achievement. Studies have found students of racially diverse teachers perform higher on math and English language arts standardized tests (Dee, 2004; Pitts, 2007).
- They form supportive relationships that influence students' nonacademic performance. Scholars found lower rates of absenteeism, reduced dropout rates, increased likelihood of graduation, and higher rates of college entry and persistence (Farkas et al., 1990; Hess & Leal, 1997).
- They often interrupt the school-to-prison pipeline by reducing disciplinary referrals and time out of school for behavioral infractions (Lindsay & Hart, 2017). Researchers suggest these findings may be connected to educators' positive perceptions of students and their potential (Decker

et al., 2007). Black and Latino/x students who are taught by educators who share their ethnic and racial background are less likely to be enrolled in special education courses and more likely to participate in gifted programs and advanced coursework (Grissom et al., 2017).

- They demonstrate a commitment to underserved communities and often work in hard-to-staff schools. Indeed, educators of color are overrepresented in urban and Title 1 schools (schools with a high percentage of students from low-income communities; Farinde-Wu et al., 2017; NCES, 2019b).
- They bridge cultural gaps between students, their families, and schools (Nevarez et al., 2019). Studies indicate many educators of color take on additional unpaid tasks such as document translation and interpretation for speakers of languages other than English (Gordon, 1997).
- They draw on an asset-based perspective of students' background knowledge and home language, often incorporating them into building blocks for learning. Many educators of color apply culturally responsive techniques in the classroom to engage their students (Quiocho & Rios, 2000).

Diversifying the educator workforce is also beneficial for students who do not identify as persons of color. Educators of color offer the following advantages for all students:

- They can be positive role models for students from different backgrounds and lived experiences. Moreover, culturally responsive techniques often used by educators of color add value to all students' learning (Blazar, 2021).
- They humanize complex issues like immigration and counter stereotypes. Students taught by educators of color report feeling more equipped to understand social problems and enter diverse settings like a college classroom (Anderson, 2015).
- They support students' cultural awareness. For instance, Ladson-Billings describes the significance of white students' exposure to Black teachers in mitigating inaccurate or incomplete understandings about communities of color (Ferlazzo, 2015). Educators of color can also create avenues for cross-racial dialogue with students (Anderson, 2015).

- Both students of color and white students report higher rates of social belonging and positive relationships with students and staff in spaces that are racially diverse (Cherng & Davis, 2017). In one study, white students ranked educators of color more favorably than they did white teachers (Cherng & Halpin, 2016).

A diverse educator workforce presents numerous opportunities to enhance all students' educational experiences. Take a moment to consider these points in the context of your own experiences. What effect did experiencing (or not experiencing) instruction from a teacher of color have on your K–12 educational experiences?

Bringing Misconceptions to the Surface

Although researchers agree that educators of color add value for their students and school communities, be careful regarding assumptions such as the following:

- Educators of color are monolithic in their approach to teaching.
- Educators of color are best equipped to teach students of color.
- Educators of color are best suited to address issues of race and injustice in school organizational contexts.
- Educators of color who share ethnic and racial backgrounds with their students also share similar life experiences.

These assumptions can lead to unspoken toxic organizational dynamics and racial tokenism.

Historical Legacy of Educators of Color in America

The benefits to diversifying the educator workforce described previously are buoyed by an exploration of the vast historical contributions of educational pioneers of color. In his work describing the history of Black education in the South, scholar James D. Anderson (1988) writes that education for the purpose of empowerment and collective uplift was a central tenet of the Black community, particularly against the backdrop of chattel slavery. Although literacy and any type of formal schooling were prohibited by white landowners, historical records reveal Black educators funded and operated a form of public school for enslaved and free Africans as early as the 1830s (prior to the adoption of public schools in the South). Following the abolishment of slavery, Black politicians were pivotal in establishing universal public schools in the U.S. South for all children, regardless of race, color, or social class.

This commitment to education from the community continued throughout the Jim Crow era. Despite inferior funding and resources, Black educators enacted a tradition of rigorous instruction and high expectations. While *de jure* segregation was illegal in many Northern states, discriminatory lending practices and residential patterns shaped racially isolated Black schools. Defying the "separate and unequal" conditions that permeated their professional (and personal) lives, prominent 19th- and 20th-century Black educators such as Anna Julia Cooper, Inez Beverly Prosser, Fanny Jackson Coppin, and Septima Poinsette Clark advanced equity and opportunity for communities denied access to the same quality of education as their white counterparts.

Similar stories abound of non-Black educators of color and their commitment to excellent teaching despite histories of forced segregation, racial prejudice, and resource scarcity. Deirdre A. Almeida (1997), a Lenni Lenape/Shawnee educator and writer, discusses American Indian resistance to schooling projects designed to "kill the Indian, save the man." Against the backdrop of assimilationist initiatives and institutions designed to "Americanize" American Indians by stripping their language and cultural practices, educators such as Ella Deloria (Aŋpétu Wašté Wiŋ) and Ruth Muskrat Bronson modeled resistance while teaching in these very institutions (Gere, 2005). Since the closing of the final Indian boarding schools in the late 20th century, a central theme in American Indian communities has been to use education to reclaim their culture and empower their members (Juneau, 2001). Asian Americans and Pacific Islanders have been historically underrepresented in the field of education, yet teaching was also encouraged in these communities as a means of resistance to discrimination, particularly during moments of heightened anti-Asian oppression (Tamura, 1995).

Rarely do the achievements of educators of color attract national attention, although a few instances have been brought to the national consciousness in the United States. The award-winning 1988 film *Stand and Deliver* portrays the efforts of Jaime Escalante, a Bolivian American educator. Working in the underfunded East Los Angeles public schools, Escalante created an accelerated math program that culminated in an Advanced Placement (AP) Calculus course. At one point, his students represented 25 to 30 percent of all Latino students sitting for the AP exam. Between 1986 and 1991, over half of his students passed the exam. Escalante often credited his program's success to high expectations combined with quality instruction:

> Kids are not born bad students; however, the school and the student's home and community environment can produce a bad student. The educator is the crucial point in this equation. It is up to the educator to bring out the *ganas* [the desire] out of the students. (Escalante & Dirmann, 1990, p. 3)

In 1995, Mexican American science educator Elsa Salazar Cade was recognized for gap-narrowing outcomes for students with disabilities from socioeconomically disadvantaged backgrounds ("In top ten of science teachers," 1995). Research conducted by a team from the University of Buffalo found that students with behavioral challenges in Salazar Cade's classroom consistently outscored district peers on standardized assessments and did not earn discipline referrals while in her class. Researchers concluded that rigorous science instruction combined with relationship building and cultural sensitivity led to her students' superior performance. Salazar Cade's ability to balance her duties as a classroom educator with an active research agenda also garnered her acclaim in the science community.

Untold in this section are the efforts of countless educators of color over the years who positively influenced academic and nonacademic outcomes for socioeconomically disadvantaged communities and children of color. There are just too many—and too many unreported—to list here. But by contextualizing efforts to diversify the educator workforce within the frame of their contributions, we honor their stories.

The Current State of the Educator Workforce

As stated previously, a large ethnic-racial imbalance exists between the student population and the educator workforce in the United States. What factors led to this imbalance? In other words, how did we get here?

In the first half of the 19th century, the teaching profession attracted primarily white, middle-class men, but a shift occurred in the second half of the century. Undergirded by the assumptions that feminine traits were better suited for teaching children and that women would be willing to work for lower wages, society encouraged unmarried white women to become teachers. Today, white, middle-class women continue to represent the largest share of the educator workforce (Ingersoll et al., 2018).

In the 19th and 20th centuries, many aspiring educators trained in normal schools (institutions targeted at teacher training), colleges, and universities. While there was great demand from communities of color for educators who shared their background, barriers such as a dearth of quality training programs that admitted candidates of color prevented that demand from being met. Despite these barriers, teaching was often a sought-after career choice in communities of color, particularly in the South, where the Black educator workforce totaled 82,000 by 1954 (Oakley et al., 2009). That same year, the *Brown v. Board of Education* ruling would mark the beginning of a decline in the number of Black educators that would continue for the next several decades as school districts complied with court-ordered integration plans. Tens of thousands of Black educators were demoted, lost their jobs as segregated Black schools were closed, or were denied employment in the newly integrated schools. By 1964, 38,000 Black educators were displaced, many of whom were more qualified to teach than their white colleagues (Oakley et al., 2009).

In the 1980s, concerns regarding the educator shortage and recognition of the rapid ethnic-racial diversification of K–12 students led to interest in fostering a more diverse educator workforce. Many states implemented workforce diversification initiatives and successfully increased the number of educators of color. From 1987 to 2012, the number increased from 325,000 to 642,000, outpacing the induction of white candidates into the profession (Ingersoll & May, 2011). This growth contradicted claims regarding a lack of qualified or interested candidates of color. However, growth has not been consistent among all ethnic and racial groups. While the share of Hispanic and Asian educators increased from 2004 to 2016, the share of Black and American Indian/Alaska Native educators decreased (see Figure 1.1).

Efforts to diversify the educator workforce have been further undermined by turnover in the profession, especially among educators of color.

FIGURE 1.1

Comparison of Teacher Composition by Race/Ethnicity, 2003-2004 Versus 2015-2016

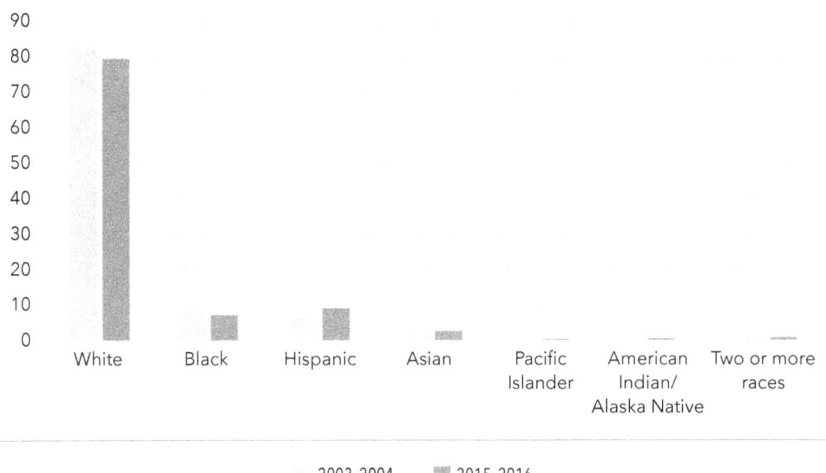

Source: From *Recruitment, Spotlight A: Characteristics of Public School Teachers by Race/Ethnicity,* by National Center for Education Statistics, 2019b, Institute of Education Sciences, U.S. Department of Education. https://nces.ed.gov/programs/raceindicators/spotlight_a.asp

Nationally representative data sets of employment trends in public and private schools from 1988 to 2009 indicate that educators of color change positions and leave teaching at higher rates than their white colleagues (see Figure 1.2). A closer analysis of turnover reveals that factors related to school organizational contexts and leadership explain these disproportionate rates of departure. An analysis of 2013 departure rates among educators of color by Ingersoll and colleagues (2021) offers insight into conditions that shape decisions to switch schools or leave altogether:

- 81 percent reported dissatisfaction with leadership behaviors.
- 65 percent were dissatisfied with school culture of standardized testing and performance-based accountability.
- 61 percent expressed dissatisfaction with student discipline problems.
- 57 percent conveyed dissatisfaction because of lack of autonomy over their classroom.
- 56 percent were dissatisfied with inferior facilities and access to resources.

Classroom interruptions, low salary, large classroom sizes, and dissatisfaction with teaching roles also factored into turnover decisions. However, these

FIGURE 1.2

Percentage of Annual Teacher Change and Departure by Minority Status and Year

	Minority Teachers			White Teachers		
Year	Moves	Leaves	Total	Moves	Leaves	Total
1988-1989	9.2	5.9	15.1	7.9	6.5	14.4
1991-1992	7.0	6.1	13.1	7.2	6.0	13.2
1994-1995	9.2	7.6	16.8	6.7	7.2	13.9
2000-2001	8.4	7.5	15.9	7.7	8.2	15.9
2004-2005	9.0	10.4	19.4	7.6	8.8	16.4
2008-2009	10.1	9.2	19.3	6.7	8.9	15.6

Source: From *Recruitment, Retention and the Minority Teacher Shortage* (Table 6), by R. M. Ingersoll and H. May, 2011, Consortium for Policy Research in Education.

reasons paled in comparison with the aspects of organizational experiences listed earlier. Nearly a decade later, reports released by The Education Trust (Dixon et al., 2019; Griffin, 2018) and Teach Plus (Mason et al., 2021) corroborated Ingersoll and colleagues' seminal findings. Accordingly, efforts to diversify the educator workforce and retain educators of color cannot be divorced from recognizing the substantial churn of educators of color and influence of schools' social organization on educator satisfaction and retention.

Principle 1: Acknowledge That Educator Diversity Matters

There is no question of the importance of educator diversity. A diversified educator workforce strengthens representation and promotes democracy, provides multiple benefits to student well-being and achievement, and acknowledges the historical contributions of unrecognized educators of color. Yet such educators still face multiple barriers in schools that lead to disproportionate turnover—an issue of great concern.

Increasing the ethnic-racial diversity of the educator workforce is not just a fashionable trend; rather, giving attention to this issue is a justice-oriented obligation. To continue with the status quo would be a disservice to all students. Successful recruitment and retention initiatives will necessitate transforming systems, institutions, policies, and most of all, school organizational conditions. We must recall and respond to Richard Riley's (1998) call to action: "If we are to be responsive to the special demands and great opportunities of our nation's pluralistic makeup, we should develop a teaching force that is diverse, as well" (p. 19).

Some reminders as this chapter draws to a close:

1. Increasing the ethnic-racial makeup of the educator workforce does not imply preferential treatment of people of color. Rather, it calls attention to rectifying the historical and contemporary systems of exclusion in education that have uniquely shaped the experiences of communities and individuals of color.
2. Diversifying the educator workforce isn't a compromise or substitute for excellent teaching and qualified candidates. Focusing on the recruitment and retention of underrepresented populations fosters wider opportunity and access, engaging more qualified educators to lead our classrooms.
3. Recruiting, hiring, and retaining educators of color are part of the larger work of reimagining our educational system through the lenses of equity, opportunity, and access. Although in earlier times education was characterized as the "great equalizer," equipping students to attain the American dream, history shows that education has been largely "separate and unequal" for centuries. Macro-level change is needed to rectify unequal systems, but change on a smaller scale can still support those efforts. The arguments and strategies in this book will help instructional leaders and instructional leadership teams advance culturally affirming conditions in their schools through concrete practices.

Conclusion

Educators of color are underrepresented in teaching and face disproportionate turnover. The principles presented in this book are geared toward instructional leaders of all backgrounds and intersections of identity whose primary job responsibilities are in educator recruitment and hiring, professional development, coaching, observation and feedback, and other supportive measures of fostering effective teaching. The everyday leadership practices and principles here can collectively advance and nurture culturally affirming conditions where educators are represented, seen, and valued.

❓ Reflection Questions

1. Consider the key themes of this chapter: urgency of educator workforce diversification, benefits associated with educators of color, and historical context for ethnic-racial imbalance. Which of these themes resonates the most with you? How might you summarize these themes to create a 30-second elevator pitch about the importance of educator diversity?
2. What are other important reasons to diversify the workforce at your school?
3. When did you have your first Black educator? Latino/x? Asian or American Indian? What lessons did you draw from their approach to teaching and learning?
4. Consider the concept of ethnic-racial diversity in the educator workforce in relation to your students. How might your students benefit from a racially, ethnically, and linguistically diverse educator workforce?
5. In what ways do the legacies of prominent educators like Anna Julia Cooper, Jaime Escalante, and the other educators of color presented in this chapter contribute to understanding the importance of a diverse educator workforce?

📚 Beyond the Text: Resources to Level Up

History of Schools and Schooling

Anderson, J. D. (1988). *The education of Blacks in the South, 1860–1935.* University of North Carolina Press.

Givens, J. R. (2021). *Fugitive pedagogy: Carter G. Woodson and the art of Black teaching.* Harvard University Press.

Spring, J. (2016). *Deculturalization and the struggle for equality: A brief history of the education of dominated cultures in the United States* (8th ed.). Routledge.

Walker, V. S. (2018). *The lost education of Horace Tate: Uncovering the hidden heroes who fought for justice in schools*. The New Press.

Diversifying the Educator Workforce

Bond, B., Quintero, E., Casey, L., & Di Carlo, M. (2015). *The state of teacher diversity in American education.* Albert Shanker Institute. https://www.shankerinstitute.org/resource/teacherdiversity

Gist, C. D., & Bristol, T. J. (2021). *Building a more ethnoracially diverse teaching force: New directions in research, policy, and practice.* Kappan. https://pdkmembers.org/members_online/publications/archive/pdf/PDK_2021_SpecialIssue/PDK_SpecialIssue_2021_CompleteIssue.pdf

Learning from Educators of Color

Barnhardt, R. (2008). Creating a place for Indigenous knowledge in education: The Alaska Native knowledge network. In D. A. Gruenewald & G. A. Smith (Eds.), *Place-based education in the global age: Local diversity* (pp. 113–133). Lawrence Erlbaum Associates.

Foster, M. (Ed.). (1997). *Black teachers on teaching*. New Press.

Kim, G. M., & Cooc, N. (2020). Teaching for social justice: A research synthesis on Asian American and Pacific Islander teachers in U.S. schools. *Teaching and Teacher Education, 94,* 103104.

Ochoa, G. L. (2007). *Learning from Latino teachers*. Jossey-Bass.

2

PRINCIPLE 2:
Cultivate Reflection and Self-Awareness

Reflection—true reflection—leads to action.
       —Paulo Freire, *Pedagogy of the Oppressed*

Decades of research document the importance of reflection and its promising effects on teaching and learning. Reflection should be viewed as an action-oriented activity that begets a change in practice. Professional learning researcher David Boud and his team (2013) characterize reflection as transformation work, describing it as

> [a] term for those intellectual and affective activities in which individuals engage to explore their experiences in order to lead to new understandings and appreciation. It may take place in isolation or in association with others. (p. 19)

Such reflection is not new to instructional leaders, who are trained to reflect on all kinds of components of their professional practice: leadership behaviors, data, best practices, management, relationship building, engagement with students' caregivers, and so much more.

Instructional leaders also understand the importance of being self-aware. Leadership coach and organizational psychologist Tasha Eurich (2018) identifies two elements to self-awareness: the first "represents how clearly we see our own values, passions, aspirations, . . . and impact on others" (para. 9), and the second involves understanding how others perceive us. Together, reflection and self-awareness are prerequisite to developing an action plan to support and retain educators of color.

This chapter addresses the extent to which reflection and self-awareness are necessary to supporting and retaining a diverse educator workforce, with guidance from real-life voices from the field of education. A set of short narratives demonstrates how educators of color implement these practices in the workplace, setting the stage for us to grapple with whether we should confront issues related to race in schools or avoid them. Following these narratives, three practical strategies are given to jump-start the work of Principle 2 in our own practice: interrogate biases, understand intent and impact, and consider intersectionality. The chapter concludes with a call to action.

How Necessary Are Reflection and Self-Awareness?

The organizational dynamics of schools and how they affect educators of color entail a peculiar paradox. Supported by local and federal policy, many schools and districts across the United States implement initiatives to diversify their educator workforce. However, as noted in Chapter 1, educators of color leave the profession at higher rates than they enter it, undermining recruitment initiatives (Ingersoll et al., 2021). As such, the desired influence of the many benefits that accompany a diverse educator workforce is diminished. Data from several sources reveal that educators of color often confront interpersonal and institutional dynamics that fail to respect and value their personhood (Campoli & Conrad-Popova, 2017; Flores, 2011; Stanley, 2021, 2022). These issues may be compounded by "hidden racism"—comments, jokes, and color-evasive strategies leading to racial climates that undermine teachers' motivation, disregard their humanity, and lead to turnover. Some scholars have reframed this phenomenon as "pushout" because of the ways organizational dynamics are unwelcoming and unsafe for educators of color (Pizarro & Kohli, 2020).

Discussing school racial climates in the context of ethnic-racial diversity can be tense. The following stories reinforce the importance of reflection and self-awareness in providing supportive and inclusive environments for educators of color. Many describe circumstances in which the narrator experienced marginalization (psychological or emotional injury due to experiencing discrimination or bias). The voices highlighted here are not intended to be representative of all educators of color, nor do the stories account for all conditions faced by educators of color or the ways in which heterosexism, ableism, and other forms of oppression can be moderated in the workplace. Inclusion of these anecdotes is not intended to pathologize communities of color but to center underrepresented voices, sparking instructional leaders to engage in the process of reflection and self-awareness themselves.

Names of contributors throughout the book are pseudonyms, and some details have been omitted or altered to preserve the anonymity of the educators who have shared their insights with me over years of interviews. Nevertheless, these anecdotes represent the types of workplace interactions and experiences that educators of color face every day.

Diane: Defined by Discipline

Diane, a Black educator with over 15 years of experience in urban schools with majority Latino/x students, is one of the most experienced teachers in her school. Her students consistently score high on both teacher-made assessments and standardized tests. Diane is well respected among colleagues for her no-nonsense approach and strong relationships with students. But although her students consistently outperform their peers in other schools, she often feels her content expertise and pedagogical skills are discounted or dismissed. She sometimes leads professional development for her history team, but she feels overlooked for leadership opportunities targeting student achievement for other educators. She expressed her frustration at being "pigeonholed" as a disciplinarian:

> As a Black woman, I'm considered to be the disciplinarian but never the leader. I'm one of the most experienced teachers in the building but the first to cover classes, the first assigned to lunch duty, or the first to attend field trips. It may not be explicitly articulated, but if [I'm] always

being called on to do specific jobs, [I] can only believe that this is the only thing that you think I can do. I can do other things aside from telling children to sit down and be quiet. I have a brain and I can teach, and kids can learn from me.

Although Diane's leadership opportunities in the school are limited, she has taken it upon herself to engage in interdisciplinary collaboration, working with other content educators (all of whom are Black) to enhance her social studies instruction and support students' critical thinking in their other courses. She also volunteered to informally coach and support younger educators, even though this unpaid labor goes unacknowledged by school leaders.

Atiq: Underestimated and Underappreciated

Nearing his fifth year in the classroom, Atiq works in a city magnet school with a racially diverse student population. Born in the United States and of Moroccan descent, he feels largely isolated from his colleagues, many of whom are white and female. He described receiving positive praise from leadership about his teaching but having mixed experiences with parents:

> I had some parents that seemed to like that their child's teacher was a young man of color. However, there were some parents that were under the impression that I was just a support teacher. They often assumed I was unqualified. One time during student orientation, I was at the door, inviting all my new students and their families into the classroom. When the parent came to the door, she asked where the classroom teacher was. When I told her that I was the teacher, she took the child's hand and walked down to the main office. Would you believe that she switched her child out of my class? That didn't feel good at all; in fact, it's demoralizing. But if she thinks I can't teach, what can I do? That wasn't the only time, either, that children were taken out of my classroom and moved to another class. However, the admin never said anything about it. It was like I was expected to just accept this from parents and move on.

Atiq's experience has been affected by the lack of administrator intervention with regard to families who are resistant to his role as their child's teacher.

Leslie: Microaggressions and Micromanagement

Leslie has been teaching for 10 years in a mix of suburban and urban settings. She spoke with great affection of her early-career experiences in suburban schools; in particular, she fondly remembered her "school mothers," all of whom were older educators who provided guidance and a listening ear in her formative years as a classroom teacher. Several years later, Leslie transferred to another school to teach reading. As a biracial woman, Leslie experienced ongoing tension with her school leaders:

> My principal, he would do things like—I'm 5 foot 3 and he's probably 6 foot 3 or taller. He would purposely stand in my space to try and create this sense of intimidation. It was like a racial microaggression but it was worse. I felt unsafe. . . . I mean, you know the message that's being sent when someone is in your [physical] space.

Leslie hoped to receive some understanding from the school's assistant principal, who is also a woman. However, Leslie found their interactions to be cold and distant. Some time later, Leslie experienced a traumatic miscarriage that caused her to take time from work. These absences were regarded as a professional shortcoming on her part. She said:

> When I had my final evaluation from my assistant principal, my miscarriage was brought up and thrown in my face. Well, it wasn't specifically mentioned, but she mentioned that certain things were left undone because I was [out of school]. At that point, I couldn't do it anymore. There was no way I could come to that.

Leslie then shared that she subsequently left teaching for several years; when she returned, she decided to change districts rather than return to the one that showed such a lack of support.

Each of these stories points out examples of ways school environments fall short regarding support and inclusivity. Diane's story raises alarms about how educators of color are often viewed as enforcers, particularly in socioeconomically disadvantaged or underperforming schools. This is especially salient in schools with high numbers of Black, Latino/x, and other students of color (Bristol & Mentor, 2018). Such additional tasks are often imposed and unpaid burdens that detract from teachers' primary responsibilities in the classroom, possibly affecting official performance evaluations. Like many in her position, Diane feels her contributions to the school community are unseen and undervalued.

In contrast, Atiq feels his teaching is valued by school leaders, but he has experienced mixed responses from parents, some of whom implicitly rejected his qualifications and competency. Atiq notes the absence of intervention from school leadership in these cases; without an explanation, he feels unsupported and undermined as a professional.

Leslie's experiences reflect the intersection of race and gender. The additional lack of care and support from administration compounded the challenging circumstances surrounding her miscarriage and ultimately influenced her decision to leave the school.

Each anecdote represents a missed opportunity for instructional leaders to address or intervene in the scenario. They failed to understand the issues at stake, acknowledge the impact of their actions or lack thereof, and course-correct. These leadership missteps—intentional or unintentional—influenced how Diane, Atiq, and Leslie experienced the workplace.

Defining Microaggressions

Author and counseling psychologist Derald Wing Sue (2010) defines microaggressions as actions and behaviors that communicate derogatory messages about a minoritized individual and/or group by a member or members of a dominant group. Although such interactions may be subtle or unintentional, researchers conclude that experiencing microaggressions can result in psychological and physical effects (Nadal et al., 2017).

Decisions to Make: Address Race in Schools or Avoid?

You may have experienced significant discomfort while reading these accounts. Considering the predominant presence of white educators in positions of leadership (NCES, 2020a), if you identify as white, you may not have had to confront racial experiences like those described here in your own career as a student or educator in K–12 schools. On the other hand, these stories may bring about discomfort because they are similar to your own observations or firsthand experiences in the workplace. The power of these real-life accounts comes from their origin in interpersonal interactions with instructional leaders or other members of the school community. The negative effects of many of these exchanges may have been unintended; after all, we presume that most people oppose unequal treatment based on race, gender, national origin, and other aspects of identity. In fact, equality is one of the underlying assumptions of the American democratic experiment. Equality is often presumed in legislation and undergirds the right to live, work, and attend school without discrimination. However, these stories contradict the notion of ubiquitous equality, leading us to a philosophical crossroads: should we confront issues related to race in schools or avoid them?

Let's consider the implications of avoiding racial issues in schools. To avoid race is to ignore the legacy of racism moderated through schooling in the United States. Even after the cessation of chattel slavery and removal of antiliteracy laws denying enslaved Africans the opportunity to learn, state-sanctioned school segregation in the South and Midwest still characterized much of the 19th and 20th centuries (see Figure 2.1). Though state legislatures in the West did not mandate racial segregation, many communities of color were implicitly required to attend separate schools (Donato & Hanson, 2012; Gándara & Orfield, 2010).

Long after the 1954 *Brown v. Board of Education* ruling abolished school segregation, studies indicate rates of de facto school segregation in the United States have begun to rise in recent decades. Drawing from longitudinal school enrollment data by region, Figure 2.2 depicts this increase in the percentage of Black students attending intensely segregated schools where 90–100 percent of students identify as Black, Latino/x, or other minoritized populations. Most often, these schools are situated in low-income communities with disproportionately lower levels of funding than more affluent, mostly white districts.

Avoiding racial issues in schools means overlooking histories of how schools have been used to oppress and subjugate communities of color. For instance, in the 19th and early 20th centuries, federally financed Indian

FIGURE 2.1

U.S. School Segregation Prior to 1954 *Brown v. Board of Education* Ruling

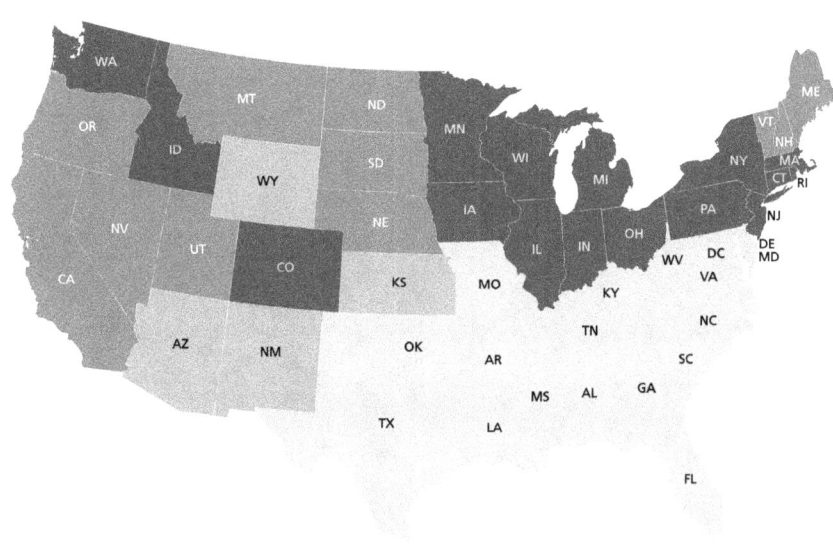

Mandatory segregation · Optional segregation · No school segregation legislation · Segregation forbidden

Source: Data from "The African American Struggle for Civil Rights: Desegregation and Integration," by Texas Higher Education Coordinating Board, n.d., Open Education Resources Repository. https://oertx.highered.texas.gov/courseware/lesson/1407/student/?task=3

boarding schools stripped Native children of their culture by removing them from their families and home communities (Spring, 2016). The educational philosophies underlying these institutions were best captured by the phrase used by Richard Henry Pratt, founder of the infamous Carlisle Indian Industrial School, to justify their existence: "Kill the Indian, save the man." Another example is the displacement and internment of Americans of Japanese descent during World War II and the requirement that these children attend under-resourced and overcrowded schools within the boundaries of internment camps.

To avoid issues of race also means ignoring how historic race-based exclusion policies correlate with sizable resource and funding inequalities that continue to disproportionately affect students of color and socioeconomically disadvantaged communities (Baker & Green, 2014). Even well-meaning attempts to treat all individuals as equally as possible (often referred to as *colorblindness*)

FIGURE 2.2

Black Students Enrolled in Schools Characterized by High Minority Population

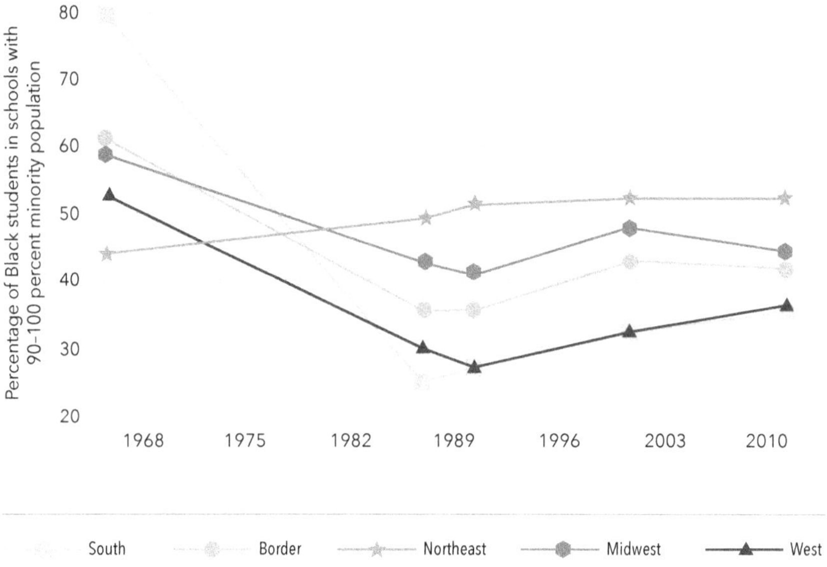

Source: From Brown *at 60: Great Progress, a Long Retreat and an Uncertain Future* (p. 18), by G. Orfield, E. Frankenberg, J. Ee, & J. Kuscera, 2014, The Civil Rights Project/Proyecto Derechos Civiles. https://www.civilrightsproject.ucla.edu/research/k-12-education/integration-and-diversity/brown-at-60-great-progress-a-long-retreat-and-an-uncertain-future

fail to address the implications of these histories and their contemporary consequences for communities of color. After all, colorblindness presumes a level playing field, incorrectly suggesting that racism in schools is now nonexistent and neglecting to uproot racism's oppressive legacy.

Several studies to date have explored the effects of colorblindness on school culture and interpersonal relationships among school personnel, students, and the broader school community. Educational scholar and consultant Eddie Fergus (2017) writes that proponents of colorblindness, in de-emphasizing the significance of race and racism, intensify its harmful repercussions. Failure to acknowledge and affirm unique social identities reproduces harm to minoritized individuals because it minimizes their everyday realities and overlooks the legacies of injury that have hurt their communities. Colorblindness, which Fergus argues "is [a] socially acceptable bias that lives in our personal and institutional beliefs" (2017, para. 6), emerges in subtle ways. For example, it often masks racial inequalities and racialized (mis)treatment. This view is supported by Rita Kohli (2018) and Ain Grooms and colleagues (2021), who argue that downplaying race or minimizing racism undermines collegiality and erodes workplace satisfaction among educators of color. They also found that colorblindness among school faculty is associated with increased turnover among educators of color and can even lead to stress and difficulty sleeping. Comments such as "I ignore skin color and try to treat everyone as individuals," "I don't see those I work with as having a race," and "We're all just the human race" are likely intended to be progressive, but they overlook and dismiss deeply entrenched inequalities. Avoiding issues of race and racism (which Howard Stevenson calls "the elephant in the room" [2014, p. 191]) negatively affects the organizational health and stability of schools. Alternatively, embracing a color-conscious approach acknowledges the historical implications of race and racism; recognizes race and racism as factors influencing the lived experiences of communities of color; and actively works to identify, dismantle, and replace harmful policies and practices in schools.

> ### Addressing the Reality of Racism and Racial Harm in Schools
> It is important to remember that efforts to address racism are not the equivalent of doing favors for people of color but a way to acknowledge historical and contemporary harms, particularly harms that occurred within educational institutions, and work to undo them. As presented in Chapter 1 and in this chapter, the role of racism in enacting inequalities and excluding communities of color did not occur by happenstance; the inequalities and exclusion were the result of educational policy and practice.

Principle 2: Cultivate Reflection and Self-Awareness

Edward Fergus (2017) writes, "No area of work is more difficult than reformulating the beliefs and worldviews of educators as school districts try to develop, implement, and monitor an equity perspective and pedagogical lens" (para. 13). Integral to this process of "reformulating beliefs and worldviews" is cultivating reflection and self-awareness, which can be accessed using the following three strategies: interrogate biases, understand intent and impact, and consider intersectionality.

Strategy 1: Interrogate Biases

Bias refers to implicit attitudes or judgments that the brain forms in relation to firsthand experiences, observations, or beliefs that are conveyed in society (Ruhl, 2023; see also Staats, 2016). A result of cognitive processing and social conditioning, biases can be directed at any aspect of identity (e.g., gender, gender expression, sexual orientation, age, religion, ability) or personal characteristics (e.g., education level).

Biases are not always bad. For example, a patient might develop a sense of safety and relief in the presence of a nurse, often portrayed in visual and print media as nurturing, kind, and caring. This impression might also be reinforced by previous experiences with nurses. Subsequently, these associations become etched in the patient's long-term memory, and a bias is formed. Biases can be problematic, however, when influenced by inaccurate or incomplete information. For example, most cultural depictions of nurses are women, not men, which may lead to biases regarding nurses and gender, and influence the patient's preferences and interactions with nurses who do not identify as women. The patient may become resistant or distrustful of male nurses, even if the patient is unconscious of the bias. I use this example to convey the point that, even if we perceive ourselves to be impartial and capable of treating others without discrimination, our cognitive processes may affect our thoughts and interactions in ways to which we are oblivious.

Studies indicate that bias has significant implications for the workplace. Emerging from personal experiences, conscious and unconscious bias may influence aspects of recruitment, hiring, promotion, support, and everyday encounters in contradiction of explicit beliefs, undermining aspirations of recruiting and retaining a diverse educator workforce. Although bias training has become more commonplace in PK–12 schools and professional development, a slew of studies indicate mixed results regarding its effectiveness. One critique is that awareness of bias may not lead to willingness to change (Noon, 2018). Following are additional reasons many disengage from bias training:

- Participants are often told, not shown. Being told about bias is insufficient to uproot unconscious attitudes. Instead, we must engage in "show and tell"; firsthand confrontations with implicit beliefs produce greater transformation than analyzing the effects of bias. In a national seminar convened by the National Institutes of Health (2021) interrogating the effectiveness of bias training, Molly Carnes reported a longitudinal study in which case studies were effectively used to facilitate participants' confrontation with their own bias. Following their involvement in the antibias program, participants reported increased awareness of bias (including the types of scenarios in which bias was likely to manifest) and motivation to mitigate the effect of bias on their daily lives. These positive results lasted for up to three years.
- Participants often comply or cooperate but may not commit. Participation in activities related to bias may be viewed as a compliance measure, because training is often professionally mandated. Instead of complying, some participants may choose to cooperate because the training aligns with their interests or they perceive it as useful. However, a one-and-done approach is not effective. To dismantle social conditioning and rework neural pathways, we must engage in interrogating our biases due to an intrinsic commitment to changing our beliefs and, subsequently, our practice. To further the effectiveness of bias training, Robert Sellers argued that it must be ongoing, be part of a larger institutional strategy to enact change, and foster individual commitment (National Institutes of Health, 2021).
- Participants incorrectly associate awareness with action. Divorced from action, awareness of bias is insufficient. Studies on this topic indicate that knowing one's biases does not prevent their effects. For example, Francesca Gino and Katherine Coffman (2021) argue that effective trainings must support participants in unearthing their own biases and changing their behavior.

The following activities are intended to facilitate the process of cultivating reflection and self-awareness regarding bias.

Racial Memory Activity

A good way to start surfacing personal biases is to consider the following questions: How old were you when you first thought about race? What did you learn? By reflecting on specific life stages, you can begin to develop a consciousness about the types of information you have internalized about race and how that information links with your biases. Start by recalling your earliest race-related memory. Using a journal or another note-taking device, describe the event in detail, including who was present, what happened, how old you were, and how you felt at the time. As you think back, consider the following: Did you talk to anyone—a parent, educator, or other caring adult—about what happened? If not, why not? What messages did you internalize about race as it related to that event?

Repeat the process for other life stages, such as elementary school, middle school, high school, college years, and beyond. Reflect on the connection between racial memories and bias by considering these questions: When did I first realize my own ethnic-racial identity? What events have shaped my understanding of my own identity? What events have shaped my understanding of other groups? To what extent have these understandings shaped my ability to understand the histories and experiences of communities of color? To what extent have these understandings been shaped by stereotypes or misinformation?

Harvard Implicit Association Test

The Harvard Implicit Association Test (Harvard IAT) is an activity often used to measure implicit attitudes on a range of topics. Like bias, implicit attitudes are positive and negative assessments and conclusions that our brains form in response to stimuli. For example, although you may say that you like to exercise (your explicit attitude), it is possible that you hold an implicit negative attitude about exercise that contradicts your explicit beliefs, and taking the Harvard IAT would indicate that your implicit attitude toward physical exercise is negative. The Harvard IAT is more tool than test; there is no pass or fail. And to be clear, the tool does not determine if someone is or is not racist. Rather, it measures test takers' response times to determine the strength of their association of concepts with negative and positive evaluations.

The Harvard IAT has received criticism, and the science is imperfect. Although it is an "effective educational tool for raising awareness about implicit bias" (Project Implicit, 2011, para. 7), one test is insufficient for diagnostic purposes. The creators of the test recommend taking it repeatedly, as exposure to stimuli may influence how you approach the test over time. Despite these limitations, the Harvard IAT lends itself to reflecting on the possibility of bias.

After taking the Harvard IAT, you may feel skepticism or disregard. The prospect of holding biases that contradict your explicit beliefs may even feel demoralizing. Others may feel justified or vindicated. You may be tempted to think about the technical aspects of the test (e.g., reaction time, hand-eye coordination, stress), but try to set those thoughts aside. It is important to reflect on your results and the factors that may have influenced any implicit associations. The Kirwan Institute for the Study of Race and Ethnicity (n.d.) suggests the following reflection questions:

- What feelings or reactions did you have upon learning your IAT results? Reflect on life experiences that may have influenced your results.
- Consider your childhood and family upbringing, the neighborhoods in which you have lived, elements of your career path, media messages, your family and peer networks, and so on. How might these experiences have shaped your biases, with or without your conscious awareness?
- How might knowing your IAT results affect your future actions and decisions, both in your role at your workplace and in other aspects of your life?

Strategy 2: Understand Intent and Impact

Intent and impact are important concepts to understand when cultivating reflection and self-awareness. *Intent* refers to underlying motivation and is characterized by the thoughts, emotions, and aspirations attached to a given situation. Conversely, *impact* refers to the actual consequences actions have for others, including how they affect others' perceptions or experiences. As instructional leaders, our intent is often well-meaning: we want to create a culture in which students thrive socioemotionally and academically, and teachers receive what is needed to manifest this vision. However, sometimes our intent does not lead to the impact we hope for. As Maura Cullen (2008) writes in *35 Dumb Things Well-Intended People Say*, "people will often make statements which they intend or perceive to be supportive or complimentary, yet end up becoming problematic" (p. 17). Guided by research, interviews with educators of color, and my own personal experiences, I have observed that actions can be equally problematic.

Here's an example of mismatch between intent and impact: "My (partner/child, sibling, best friend) is (Black, Latino/x, Asian, biracial, Native American), so I understand." How would you characterize the intent of the speaker's comment? And what possible impact(s) can you imagine the comment would have?

The intent behind the comment is probably to convey solidarity. The speaker wants to communicate that they "get it" due to their proximity to people of minoritized backgrounds. Despite the efforts to foster commonality, such comments overlook the historical and social context of identity and minimize others' experiences. They also lump all individuals from a specific ethnic-racial group together and assume they all think and feel the same way. Instead of strengthening interpersonal bonds, such comments may widen the divide. Moreover, the speaker may be unaware of the negative impact of their statement. Worse yet, they may become defensive or dismissive if confronted (e.g., responding with, "Relax! You know what I meant"). However, these actions may only serve to further fracture the relationship. For these reasons, understanding the intent and impact of your words and actions is foundational to productive interactions, particularly when engaging across the lines of ethnic-racial difference.

Let's consider a counterpoint. Some assert that we cannot control the impact of our actions on others. Given the busyness of day-to-day activities and urgency to advance student learning, they posit that leaders lack energy and capacity to scrutinize their words and actions through the lens of intent and impact. But understanding intent and impact sets a necessary context for culturally affirming practices and systems. We only need to re-examine the experiences shared by Diane, Atiq, and Leslie to see how this strategy is beneficial.

It may be the case that leadership opportunities were not intentionally withheld from Diane. In fact, her school's leaders may have perceived that her greatest contribution to the school was her ability to work with students who were often disruptive in other classes. However, the actual impact of the dearth of opportunities presented was that she did not feel valued for her intellectual or pedagogical contributions as a veteran educator, despite her record of facilitating high student achievement. Despite the intentions of her leaders, Diane's experience left her feeling the brunt of a racial stereotype that educators of color are best equipped to work with students of color.

Atiq's administrators may have intended to schedule a meeting to discuss how he had been treated by families and then merely forgot. For Atiq, however, the absence of leadership support in navigating relationships with parents left him feeling unsupported—and this lack of support contradicted the repeated praise he received from school leadership.

Leslie felt the large and looming physical presence of her leader in her space to be undergirded by sexism and racism, which may not have been his intent. The impact of these interactions, however, left her feeling vulnerable and anxious. Taken together with comments about her miscarriage that she interpreted as unkind and uncaring, Leslie perceived that she was not welcome. Ultimately, she attributed her departure to the impact of leadership's actions.

Understanding intent and impact requires vulnerability and humility in acknowledging how our well-meaning words and actions can harm others as well as reproduce the types of marginalization and oppression that occur on the basis of ethnic-racial identity, gender, or other markers of identity. Understanding intent and impact also requires bravery. For many individuals, the gut reaction to learning the consequences of intent and impact is to maintain silence out of fear of appearing prejudiced. Instead, we must reframe our thinking to understand that we are all growing in knowledge and practice to become culturally affirming practitioners. If we internalize our expanded comprehension of the impact of our words and actions as making us bad people, we inhibit opportunities for future growth. Instead, we need to lean into discomfort and process unintended impacts as learning opportunities.

The following activities are intended to facilitate the process of cultivating reflection and self-awareness by helping you examine potential gaps between intent and impact.

Intent and Impact Scenarios

Figure 2.3 presents some scenarios that are worth examining in the context of intent and impact. As you read the first two rows, reflect on any relevance between the scenarios and your own personal/professional experiences and observations. Continue with the subsequent scenarios, jotting down what may be the speaker's intent and potential impact on the listener.

FIGURE 2.3
Intent and Impact Scenarios

Comment	Intent	Impact
That name is very challenging to pronounce. Can I call you . . . ?	The speaker may not want to offend by mispronouncing a person's given name incorrectly.	Communicates lack of effort or diminished importance of learning the correct pronunciation of a person's given name.
As a woman (or "having grown up in poverty," "as a person who identifies as queer," etc.), I've also been marginalized and know how you feel.	The speaker is seeking solidarity with a member of a minoritized group by highlighting an aspect of their identity that is also stigmatized.	Generalizes marginalization by conveying that all oppression occurs by the same methods and is experienced the same way. Ignores how identity is nuanced and corresponds with intersections of power and privilege.
I hate it when that happens to me, too!		
Where are you from? Where are you really from?		
You speak [language] really well!		
I think you are reading too much into that situation.		
It was just a joke!		

Closing the Gap Between Intent and Impact

Consider the following three steps as you begin the work of closing the gap between intent and impact.

1. *Accept responsibility for action . . . or inaction.* Educators seeking to understand intent and impact must first acknowledge how their

words and actions affect others. As we saw with Atiq, failure to act can also have detrimental consequences. When confronted, listen without judgment, acknowledge the impact you had, and communicate how you commit to doing better in the future. If you suspect that you may have had a negative impact on someone, gather feedback from a person or people proximal to the encounter.

2. *Challenge your intent.* Examine what you believe your intentions to be, either in the moment or afterward. To facilitate this process, ask yourself, *What did I intend in this situation? How was my intent emblematic of bias? Do my thoughts and actions reflect potential areas of bias that I have not previously considered? What connections can I draw between my own position and this blind spot?* Reflecting on these questions can be coupled with revisiting Strategy 1 to reflect on biases that may have not been detected previously.

3. *Enhance cultural competence.* Drawing from Denboba (1993), the Georgetown University Center for Child and Human Development (n.d.) defines cultural competence as "a set of values, behaviors, attitudes, and practices within a system, organization, program or among individuals and which enables them to work effectively cross culturally. Further, it refers to the ability to honor and respect the beliefs, language, interpersonal styles and behaviors of individuals and families receiving services, as well as staff who are providing such services" (para. 21). To this end, educate yourself on the histories of communities that differ from your own background. Learn about their achievements, values, beliefs, contributions, and aspirations and the challenges they have faced. As you explore, allow your newly acquired learning to disrupt—and replace—the biases and stereotypes you once held.

Strategy 3: Consider Intersectionality

At their core, efforts to diversify the educator workforce are grounded in racial justice. The NEA Center for Social Justice (2021) defines racial justice as, "The systematic fair treatment of people of all races, resulting in equitable opportunities and outcomes for all." They continue to characterize racial justice as "not just the absence of discrimination and inequities, but also the presence of deliberate systems and supports to achieve and sustain racial equity through proactive and preventative measures" (para. 26). However, pursuit of racial justice cannot be divorced from addressing other forms of inequity and discrimination that undermine equality. Social science researchers and theorists define this as *intersectionality*. Drawn from her seminal research exploring the overlap of sexism and racism in the legal arena, Kimberlé Crenshaw portrays intersectionality as a lens to understand the complex relationship between multiple identities, power, and marginalization. In conversation with Columbia Law School reporters, Crenshaw states, "It's not simply that there's a race problem here, a gender problem here, and a class or LBGTQ problem there" ("Kimberlé Crenshaw . . . ," 2017, para. 6). Crenshaw draws on intersectionality to explain how oppression is not unilateral; rather, it can be compounded by the presence of overlapping systems that reproduce multiple types of inequality all at the same time.

Some schools attempt to embed awareness of intersectionality in their professional culture by encouraging educators to bring their whole selves to the workplace, but that raises the question of whether the workplace is a safe environment for educators of color to do so. For educators with multiple minoritized identities, this may not be the case. Shanika, a midcareer educator, described her experiences as a Black woman working at a suburban preschool. She recalled multiple instances of being singled out for wearing her hair in braids and the fit of her clothing, both of which were violations of the school's dress code. Shanika was often frustrated that her slimmer, white colleagues could wear similar clothing yet because of a difference in physique, "I would get talked to, but they wouldn't, because they are all straight up and down." Even when she chose to take her braids out and wear her hair naturally, she was admonished because the organizational handbook required all teachers wear "neat hair," a highly subjective expectation up to the school leader's interpretation.

Shanika's stories are not unique. In her study exploring experiences of 218 educators of color, Rita Kohli (2018) uncovered instances in which teachers of color were incorrectly and disproportionately reprimanded for violation of school policies. Kohli described one teacher who was scolded for wearing clothing with a logo presumed to be affiliated with a local gang. Although the teacher identified the logo as that of a baseball team, she was sent home to change. However, school leadership declined to discipline a white colleague for wearing clothing with the same logo. These examples highlight how examining race and gender together helps deepen our understanding of policies and practices that undermine the formation of culturally affirming organizational contexts. Additional considerations include ethnicity (e.g., calling educators of color by the incorrect ethnic name, imposing Western nicknames because ethnic names are perceived to be too difficult to pronounce for monolingual English speakers), age (e.g., minimizing concerns or competency of early-career teachers of color due to perceived lack of experience), and language (e.g., overreliance on multilingual educators of color to serve outside their professional capacities as informal translators).

Leaders seeking to incorporate an intersectional lens in their work can cultivate reflection and self-awareness by examining their own identities (see Appendix A for the Social Identity Reflection Tool) and considering their relationship to privilege, power, and marginalization. The Harvard Implicit Association Test discussed in Strategy 1 can also advance reflection and self-awareness regarding the intersection of race and identity markers such as religion, skin tone, and weight, to name a few. After taking the IAT, leaders can assess their own personal comfort level by engaging with others different from themselves, asking such questions as the following:

- What assumptions do I make about [identity marker]?
- How do these assumptions influence the ways I provide support?
- How comfortable am I working with individuals of diverse backgrounds?
- To what extent am I aware of intersections of identity and how they manifest in diverse needs and concerns?
- What are my views about [identity marker] and how do those views affect my attitudes about this demographic?
- What common stereotypes have I been exposed to, and to what extent do I believe these to be true or false?

Another intersectionality-focused activity is the "Father–Son Riddle." Take a moment to ponder the following riddle (Barlow, 2014; Belle et al., 2021):

> A father and son are in a horrible car crash that kills the dad. The son is rushed to the hospital; just as he's about to go under the knife, the surgeon says, "I can't operate—that boy is my son!" Explain. (Barlow, 2014, para. 1)

What was your answer? Did you conclude that the surgeon was the child's mother?

In two separate studies conducted by Brown University psychologists with over 300 participants, fewer than one-third of respondents considered the possibility that the surgeon may be a woman (Barlow, 2014). Although more creative and gender-inclusive possibilities could also qualify, the intentions of this activity are to prompt respondents to consider how the prospect of a woman surgeon is often overlooked. In fact, responses more often identified the surgeon as a father-type (e.g., adoptive father, father in a same-sex relationship, etc.) than as a woman. These findings convey that the characteristics and prestige associated with being a surgeon are often incorrectly gendered as masculine attributes. The gender reverse of this riddle may also apply (a mother and daughter are in a horrible car crash that kills the mother, and a nurse declines to attend to the victim, saying that the girl was the nurse's daughter). In this last scenario, few might guess that the attending nurse was the girl's father.

This activity can be accomplished independently or collaboratively. Following the activity, allow independent processing time to consider the following questions:

- What factors shaped how I thought about and answered this riddle?
- In what ways have my personal experiences and observations influenced the stereotypes I hold about gender?
- What mental images came to mind during this activity? How do these mental images reflect unconscious associations I hold about the intersection of gender, sexual orientation, and/or other intersections of identity?

Leaders can also analyze the effects of policy and practice on intersecting identities. For example, leaders can read organizational materials and workplace policies (e.g., dress code, maternity leave, code of conduct) and ask, *Is my school actively welcoming everybody? To what extent do policies enact safe spaces for everyone to take part?* It is also important to consider the intended audience for these policies. Who benefits, intentionally and unintentionally? Who is unaccounted for? How can they be included? When reflecting on policies, consider the range of identity markers (e.g., race, ethnicity, gender,

gender orientation, age). Remember that some identities are visible while others may be invisible (e.g., mixed race status, sexual orientation). Consider identities individually and with regard to intersectionality, and aim to move from merely including intersectionality in your reflection to placing intersectionality at the forefront of your work.

Call to Action

So what happens now? Will you avoid issues related to race in your school? Or will you take on the personal, uncomfortable, yet rewarding work of introspection coupled with policy and practice change to foster a work environment that is culturally affirming and inclusive of racially diverse educators? The purpose of this book is to equip instructional leaders with concrete, research-based culturally affirming practices, helping you to design workplaces that appeal to and retain educators of color, who are vastly underrepresented due to historical and contemporary policies and practices of exclusion and marginalization. The undergirding assumption is that reflection and self-awareness are prerequisite to efforts to diversify the educator workforce. Specifically, reflection and self-awareness will help you evaluate your own role and positionality in this work. Diversity efforts cannot—and do not—simply emerge from a place of emotional solidarity or sympathy: action is required. There is a collective responsibility to cultivate reflection and self-awareness in light of the ethical obligation to foster schools that are culturally affirming and inclusive.

Conclusion

At the beginning of this chapter, I posed several questions to establish the context for cultivating reflection and self-awareness. We considered the significance of race and racism in shaping the contemporary experiences of educators of color, some of whom have shared experiences that are sprinkled throughout the chapter. Their experiences did not occur in a silo; instead, they are connected to the ways race and racism have shaped K–12 schools throughout history. Therefore, we must ask, *Do we address issues of race in schools or do we avoid them?* To avoid race is to put on the blinders of colorblindness, muting historical realities and their effects on communities of color today. Instead, stories must be acknowledged, and new antiracist policies and practices must be enacted in workplaces to ensure "not just the absence of discrimination and inequities, but also the presence of deliberate systems and supports to achieve and sustain racial equity through proactive and preventative measures" (NEA Center for Social Justice, 2021, para. 26). I offer three strategies to achieve these ends: interrogate biases, understand intent and impact, and consider intersectionality. In the next chapter, we will build upon the foundation of reflection and self-awareness to develop an actionable plan to address elements of your school's instructional culture and your own practice.

Reflection Questions

1. This chapter highlights teacher voices from the field. What stands out for you from the stories shared by Leslie, Atiq, and Diane?
2. This chapter raises several important questions, one of which is *Should we confront issues related to race in schools, or should we avoid them?* Pinpoint a previous interaction, event, or observation in your school (or another professional context) when issues of race or racism emerged. Then reflect: What was the context surrounding that event? Who was present? What happened, and what was each participant's response? What did the event reveal about how issues related to race and racism are navigated in your school context?
3. Why is it important for you to investigate your biases? How might investigating bias help you personally and professionally?
4. Revisit the scenarios presented in Figure 2.3. How does understanding intent and impact behind these comments elucidate how well-meaning interactions can be problematic?
5. What types of inequalities have you observed (or experienced) in the workplace? How are these inequalities related to ethnic-racial identity, gender, sex and sexual orientation, language, or other markers of identity? What can you do to enhance your awareness of intersectional inequalities and minimize their effects in the workplace?

Beyond the Text: Resources to Level Up

Colorblindness

Fergus, E. (2017). Confronting colorblindness. *Phi Delta Kappan, 98*(5), 30–35.

Interrogating Bias

Fiarman, S. (2016, November 1). Unconscious bias: When good intentions aren't enough. *Educational Leadership, 74*(3), 10–15. https://www.ascd.org/el/articles/unconscious-bias-when-good-intentions-arent-enough

Kirwan Institute for the Study of Race and Ethnicity. (n.d.). *Implicit bias module series.* https://kirwaninstitute.osu.edu/implicit-bias-training

Milner, H. R., IV. (2017, December 1). Confronting inequity/Unconscious bias hurts. *Educational Leadership, 75*(4), 86–87. https://www.ascd.org/el/articles/unconscious-bias-hurts

Stevenson, H. C. (2014). *Promoting racial literacy in schools: Differences that make a difference.* Teachers College Press.

Intent and Impact

Cullen, M. (2008). *35 dumb things well-intended people say: Surprising things we say that widen the diversity gap.* Wordclay.

Inclusologists-DC. (2018, August 20). *Intention vs. impact.* YouTube. https://www.youtube.com/watch?v=83KMiek0E8I

Michigan ASCD. (2020). *Micro vs. macro-aggressions* [Virtual workshop]. http://michiganascd.org/product/micro-vs-macro-agressions/

Intersectionality

Adichie, C. (2009). *The danger of a single story.* TED. https://www.ted.com/talks/chimamanda_ngozi_adichie_the_danger_of_a_single_story/

National Association of Independent Schools. (2018, June 22). *Kimberlé Crenshaw: What is intersectionality?* YouTube. https://www.youtube.com/watch?v=ViDtnfQ9FHc

TED. (2016, December 7). *The urgency of intersectionality | Kimberlé Crenshaw.* YouTube. https://www.youtube.com/watch?v=akOe5-UsQ2o&t=36s

3

PRINCIPLE 3:
Assess and Plan for Action

Not everything that is faced can be changed, but nothing can be changed until it is faced.

—James Baldwin

Diversity is a fact, but inclusion is a choice we make every day. As leaders, we have to put out the message that we embrace and not just tolerate diversity.

—Nellie Borrero

Having grounded ourselves in the significance of this work, we now pivot to more concrete steps to help us support and retain a diverse teacher workforce: assessing and planning for action. The first step is to examine foundational elements of organizational conditions at schools that successfully support and retain teachers of color. Next, we will explore a set of tools and processes that instructional leaders can use to assess school organizational conditions and their capacity to be culturally affirming workplaces. Finally, we will look at how to apply the information gathered to developing an action plan. Along the way, we will draw on research, best practices, and voices from the field to comprehend how school organizational conditions influence the lived experiences of educators of color.

Foundational Elements of Schools

To assess readiness for supporting and retaining educators of color, we need to examine four elements: school vision and mission, leadership culture, staff dynamics, and instructional culture. This section discusses how each element contributes to the overall assessment of organizational conditions and empirical findings that underscore why these foundational elements matter.

School Vision and Mission

Coherent *school vision and mission* statements are often the focal point for what teachers, students, and community members believe—and strive to accomplish—regarding education. Such statements are the centrifugal force shaping organizational dynamics. Ideally, a school's vision and mission should guide school priorities while maintaining a laserlike focus on the effects of those priorities on students. Speaking to the importance of school vision statements, principal consultant Robyn Jackson (2021) says:

> The right vision gives you and your staff focus. It helps you determine what work you should be doing and what work you can ignore. It helps you determine whether or not you're making progress and how you should adjust if you are not. Without the right vision, it's easy to become distracted by every new mandate that comes your way. You become vulnerable to every new crisis, unmoored by every new challenge, and soon drift off course. (para. 5)

Many vision and mission statements focus on student outcomes like proficiency on standardized assessments, postsecondary success, or even intangibles such as fulfilling one's potential (Allen et al., 2018). School organizations set their vision and mission as a polestar for actualizing the purpose of education within their context and shaping adult behaviors, learning, and interactions with each other and students. Incorporating culturally affirming practices in your school's vision and mission statements is integral to creating a supportive school environment.

Organizations that support and retain teachers of color build on efforts to ensure all children and communities have access to equitable opportunities, educational excellence, and individual and collective wellness. Leaders of these schools do not conflate equity with compelling catchphrases or mantras. Rather, they pursue a vision of intersectional justice and advance this vision in every nook and cranny of the school. Educators of color are often drawn to schools with embodied visions that align with their own values and aspirations for teaching (Mason et al., 2021).

Although academic preparation is a core function of schools, Allen and colleagues (2018) find that increasing numbers of schools also promote such topics as personal development and mental wellness in their vision and mission statements. In fact, the Organisation for Economic Co-operation and Development (2018) argues that schools often overemphasize academic excellence at the expense of students' well-being (see also Allen & Kern, 2018). Many educators have shared with me in interviews that, despite being initially drawn to their school because of its aspirations for excellence, they found that the vision and mission statements were often used to impose or justify unsustainable workloads and toxic learning conditions for the sake of advancing student achievement. Of central concern was how teachers of color were expected to take on the burden of advancing student achievement by being tasked with the most difficult students or large classrooms without resources or supports. When teachers raised these concerns to school leaders, they went unheard. Accordingly, it is critical to consider the ways school vision and mission statements might be deployed to bolster or undermine efforts to support and retain educators of color.

Leadership Culture

A large and growing body of literature regarding educator diversity links turnover among teachers of color to job-related dissatisfaction with school organizational conditions (Ingersoll et al., 2021). Central to this discussion are policies, procedures, and practices instituted and governed by school leaders (Ingersoll et al., 2021; Stanley, 2021). Therefore, we must examine how leadership is defined and operationalized, and analyze implications for the broader school community.

In some schools, *leadership* refers to the school administrators: the principals and assistant principals who run the school. Other schools expand leadership to include district personnel who develop policies and procedures often executed at the school level. For our purposes, we will examine leadership in the context of instructional leaders, that is, personnel responsible for recruiting, hiring, supporting, and retaining educators of color. The definition of instructional leadership is school-specific; it often includes the school principal and assistant principal but may also encompass grade and content leaders, instructional coaches, and others. Developing a set of shared behaviors for all instructional leaders in the school is helpful for instituting culturally affirming practices to support and retain educators of color.

Much of the existing leadership literature focuses on the interplay of leadership behaviors that positively correlate with workplace satisfaction and teacher retention. Regarding instructional leadership, Joseph Blase and Jo Blase (1998, 2000) find that leaders who are visible in classrooms and common spaces, foster teacher growth, demonstrate credibility, uphold a learning-focused environment, display appreciation for teachers' efforts, and nurture educators' personal and professional needs correlate with positive workplace experiences. Mistreatment such as psychological and emotional abuse, surveillance, lack of trust, intersectional violence (e.g., racism, sexism), and absence of care predict teacher departure (Blase et al., 2008). Mistreatment can be subtle; for example, colorblindness may negatively affect the psychological and emotional well-being of educators of color.

Similar to the importance of teachers of color to students, leaders of color matter to teachers of color. Preliminary findings indicate teachers of color report higher levels of workplace satisfaction and higher levels of retention when working with principals who reflect their ethnic-racial background (Bartanen & Grissom, 2019). At the risk of oversimplifying the concept of ethnic-racial match between teachers and leaders, these findings are often attributed to the sensitivity that leaders of color bring in terms of discerning organizational conditions, understanding effects of policies and practices on minoritized teachers and students, and engaging in advocacy needed to secure a welcoming environment for all school personnel and community members.

In my own research, I have found that teachers of color are drawn to leaders who cultivate reflection and self-awareness of their own positionality considering the social context where they work. These leaders may include individuals of the same race, but they can also be leaders from different ethnic-racial backgrounds. Solange, a middle grades teacher in the Midwest, greatly admired the white leaders she described as "doing the work." She told me that her school leaders visibly cultivate reflection and self-awareness of their intersectional identities through school-based professional learning and activities outside of the school. She explained that leaders often interrogated how the mismatch between their backgrounds and the communities they served required them to lead with humility and center the voices of educators of color and community members to ensure that the school policies, procedures, and practices accommodated the voices and priorities of those who know students best.

Nathalia made similar observations. An experienced math teacher, she moved across the country from a charter school with predominantly Black and Latino/x educators to a new school where leadership did not reflect the predominantly Black and Latino/x student population. Initially wary about the implications of ethnic-racial and cultural mismatch, Nathalia observed over time that her school's leaders were aware of their cultural differences. They worked hard to get input from parents and community members about the curriculum and held regular listening and feedback sessions about school policies. When they said they were going to do something, they followed through. When unable to follow through, their missteps were named and not brushed under the rug. Nathalia recognized that all leadership has shortcomings but thought highly of her leaders because they made themselves accountable to students, teachers, and community members.

Staff Dynamics

Research findings from Glenda Flores (2011), Marcos Pizarro and Rita Kohli (2020), Darrius Stanley (2022), and others point to the influence of staff dynamics in schools that support and retain a diverse teacher workforce. *Staff dynamics* refers to the attitudes, behaviors, and relationships displayed by educators and nonteaching employees. Of central importance is how intersections of identity are moderated in interracial and intraracial interactions among colleagues, students, and the broader school community. Assessing organizational readiness to support and retain educators of color requires a critical examination of the demographic composition of staff as well as asking questions such as the following:

- Are staff racially diverse?
- Do staff represent a broad scope of positionalities, experiences, and worldviews?
- To what extent do staff reflect the students and communities they serve? If there is marked difference, what are the explicit and implicit values and beliefs of staff, and how do these values and beliefs manifest in efforts related to students?
- How do staff values and beliefs manifest in classroom pedagogy?
- How do staff values and beliefs influence interactions with students and their communities?
- How do staff values and beliefs influence interactions and relationships among staff across the lines of ethnic-racial difference?

All of these questions are critical to reflecting on staff dynamics and how they shape broader organizational conditions.

Staff who, regardless of their background, recognize the historical and contemporary implications of systemic inequality and strive to create classrooms that reflect and challenge minoritized students are necessary to organizational contexts supporting and retaining teachers of color (Kohli, 2018; Mason et al., 2021). Such staff are not just "well-meaning" or "liberal" teachers, but ones who eschew racialized assumptions that grit and hard work are sufficient to overcome institutional barriers facing communities of color. They actively seek to uproot their internalized implicit associations to facilitate respectful and healing learning environments for their students (Love, 2019). They view students as individuals with unbounded potential and take on the responsibility of crafting conditions that allow students to express their genius (Muhammad, 2020). Conversely, staff dynamics in which deficit-based values and beliefs about minoritized communities are manifest both in educator–student interactions and closed-door conversations are organizational red flags.

Bias is central to the discussion of staff dynamics, and published studies on the topic of bias among teachers abound. Findings reveal that teachers' explicit and implicit bias negatively affects student learning (Diamond et al., 2004), instructional quality (Jacoby-Senghor et al., 2016), and future educational attainment (Gershenson et al., 2016), thus widening achievement and opportunity gaps between students of color and low-income students, and their white and more affluent counterparts (Ferguson, 2003). Bias is also manifest in heightened disproportionate discipline among Black, Latino/x, and Native American students (Fergus, 2019; Skiba et al., 2022). Even high-achieving minoritized students may experience imposter syndrome, tokenism, racial microaggressions, and model minority stereotypes, all of which have significant implications for students' psychological and emotional well-being (Lee, 1994).

Findings by Yukari Amos (2020), Hilton Kelly (2007), Rita Kohli (2018), and others reveal that educators of color are not immune to their colleagues' bias. As mentioned in earlier chapters, educators of color face barriers in their attempts to advocate for students, implement cultural approaches to learning, and prove their competency and qualifications as professionals (Gabbadon, 2022). Bias may also be compounded in contexts where educators of color are positioned as disciplinarians (Bristol & Mentor, 2018) or perceived to be less valuable than white educators (Curry-Stevens & Lopezrevoredo, 2015).

In an interview with me, Mo described how she perceived racial bias as a factor influencing staff dynamics in her school:

> In my school, there is a clear racial hierarchy when it comes to staff. All nonteaching assistants and teacher assistants are folk of color, and all teachers are white except for me and one colleague. Teaching assistants are there to provide small-group and individualized support to students, but they are often asked to make copies, cover at the front desk, or complete other menial tasks. Sometimes my colleagues even get mad when my peers of color refuse to do their work for them. After all, they are there to support students—not serve at the whims of our colleagues!

Such examples of bias highlight the importance of addressing bias to improve staff's and students' experiences in schools and foster organizational conditions in which educators of color can present their full selves.

Instructional Culture

Consistent findings regarding turnover suggest three common elements that retain educators of color: support and mentoring, classroom autonomy, and opportunities for leadership and advancement. While these elements are critical to workplace satisfaction for educators of all backgrounds, qualitative and quantitative studies confirm that schools that successfully retain teachers of color intentionally address these aspects of school *instructional culture.*

Instructional Support and Mentoring

Schools that successfully retain teachers of color have proactive support strategies that align with teachers' personal values and goals. Findings from a nationwide study of educators of color reveal that they are most likely to stay in their position when they sense leaders are invested in their growth and striving to provide targeted and tangible supports (Bednar & Gicheva, 2019). Analyses of successful models found that educators who do not receive instructional support that is individualized, goal-oriented, consistent, and predictable, particularly during their early career years, are more likely to leave than those who do (Carver-Thomas, 2018). Such support may include professional development, feedback and observation loops, coteaching, coplanning, data analysis, writing assessments, or access to high-quality resources. These supports may be provided by instructional leaders directly or in partnership with universities or not-for-profit organizations. For example, organizations such as Mirrors in Education (www.mirrorsineducation.org) and the Center for Black Educator Development (www.thecenterblacked.org) deliver instructional support targeted to educators of color.

Mentoring is also linked with workplace satisfaction (Harris et al., 2007). Mentorship may take on many forms, including but not limited to an induction program pairing veteran educators with early-career educators or educators with similar interests. Mentoring relationships can form within and across schools or even districts. Local and national programs such as the Melanated Educators Collective (www.melanatededucatorscollective.com) are powerful tools leaders can use to facilitate formative relationships among educators of color, so that even schools that lack the internal capacity to offer instructional support and connections can help educators of color navigate organizational dynamics in their schools.

Classroom Autonomy

Educators of color often bring culturally responsive and innovative instructional strategies into the classroom. These instructional practices are associated with increased student engagement, motivation, and academic achievement among students of color (Ladson-Billings, 1994). Although educators of color are often recruited in hope of improving student achievement, they may face resistance to their use of cultural approaches to teaching and learning. In addition, schools based around mandated curricula and standardized testing often limit teachers' autonomy over classroom decisions, thus obscuring the experiential knowledge and agency educators of color have as professionals (Achinstein & Ogawa, 2012).

Conversely, schools that retain educators of color protect educator autonomy (Achinstein et al., 2010). These institutions welcome the ways educators of color implement culturally responsive techniques and trust educators as pedagogical experts who are knowledgeable about serving their students' needs (Achinstein & Ogawa, 2012; Dixon et al., 2019).

Opportunities for Leadership and Advancement

Schools that successfully support and retain teachers of color provide them with equitable opportunities for leadership and advancement. Rita Kohli and Marcos Pizarro (2016) found that educators of color report frequently being overlooked for leadership opportunities in their school contexts. Educators of color felt as if their advocacy for students or failure to assimilate to dominant norms limited opportunities to put their talent and skills to use. Abiola Farinde and colleagues (2016) found need for greater financial security and opportunities for advancement was linked to teacher turnover among Black women, as well as their departure from education to more viable career paths. Collectively, these studies outline the critical role of equitable access to leadership and advancement for teachers of color and the need to evaluate intersectional inequalities in the availability of opportunities.

Getting Ready to Assess and Plan for Action

Developing a culturally affirming organizational context occurs neither in a vacuum nor overnight. Assessing the state of your organization and making plans to act involves five steps: conducting prework, assessing the landscape, gathering additional information, analyzing findings, and developing an action plan.

While we focus here on instructional leaders as critical figures in advancing culturally affirming practices, you can achieve even greater capacity and accountability for this work by working with a partner, instructional team, or wider leadership team. As you move forward, it may help to assemble a group that represents a variety of perspectives on and awareness of school organizational conditions.

Step 1: Conduct Prework

Conducting prework entails compiling various types of data and anecdotal evidence in an initial assessment. Much of these data may be quantitative, but qualitative data can flesh out a multidimensional perspective. To begin, collect data that provide key insights to your school environment regarding vision and mission, leadership culture, staff dynamics, and instructional culture. Figure 3.1 shows the types of data that are helpful in this step.

Step 2: Assess the Landscape

Assessing the landscape includes completing a school culture survey to reflect on benefits and barriers to recruiting and retaining educators of color. Use the School Readiness Tool in Figure 3.2 to review the data you collected. First, rank your school on the statements in the left-hand column using a five-point scale, then reflect on or discuss with others the questions in the right-hand column.

FIGURE 3.1
Examples of Data to Collect

Vision and Mission	Leadership Culture	Staff Dynamics	Instructional Culture
Vision and mission statements	Leadership roster, including key demographic information (e.g., ethnic-racial identity, years of experience, years of tenure)	Staff roster, including key demographic information (e.g., ethnic-racial identity, years of experience, years of tenure)	Instructional guidebooks
Relevant symbols and artifacts (e.g., school mascot)			Book lists
			Curricula overview or at-a-glance documents
		Staff handbook	

FIGURE 3.2
School Readiness Tool

Vision and Mission

Your school believes in and supports every student's limitless future.	1 ☐ Not at all	2 ☐ A little	3 ☐ Some	4 ☐ A lot	5 ☐ 100%

- How does your school (through its vision and mission) demonstrate your belief in every student's full potential to do well in school and in life? How do you recognize and encourage this?
- How do you ensure the ability of Black and Brown students to achieve academically is not underestimated and that they are not overdisciplined?
- How do you oppose racist assumptions about the basic potential of students based on their racial identities and language competency?

What your school believes and values is known to your educators, students, and families.	1 ☐ Not at all	2 ☐ A little	3 ☐ Some	4 ☐ A lot	5 ☐ 100%

- What are the shared beliefs and values of your school community?
- If you had to prioritize, how would you do so? What factors influenced your prioritization?
- To what extent are these beliefs and values well known and understood by your school community? How do you know this?

Leadership Culture

Educators, students, and families have full confidence in our leadership to advance the changes we need to recruit and retain educator-activists of color.	1 ☐ Not at all	2 ☐ A little	3 ☐ Some	4 ☐ A lot	5 ☐ 100%

- Who are the leaders in your school setting? How would you describe their leadership style? How do they hold themselves accountable to student success and educator excellence?
- To what extent do school leaders represent the students, families, and communities they serve? How do they accommodate divergent perspectives and opinions when making major decisions?
- How do school leaders provide opportunities for educator leadership and voice and determine which educators may be involved in these opportunities?

Families and other school community members feel welcome and valued.	1 ☐ Not at all	2 ☐ A little	3 ☐ Some	4 ☐ A lot	5 ☐ 100%

- Who do you consider to be prominent representatives of your school culture, beyond your administration and faculty?
- How do you continuously create opportunities for voices from the margins to be included in the design process for new protocols and systems for your school?
- To what extent are families and community members an integral part of your school culture? How do you actively communicate, engage, and partner with them? How do you involve them in major decisions? What have you done recently to further engage families and communities?

Staff Dynamics

Educators mirror the students they teach in their racial identities, life experiences, and worldviews.	1 ☐ Not at all	2 ☐ A little	3 ☐ Some	4 ☐ A lot	5 ☐ 100%

- How would you describe your faculty and staff? What is the breakdown by racial identity, gender, sexual orientation, and age range? By grade and subject matter? By experience, expertise, and tenure? By salaries/benefits? By turnover rates?
- What percentage of your administration, faculty, and staff are educators of color?
- To what extent do school employees represent the racial identities and cultural backgrounds of your school's students, families, and community?
- How likely is it for a student to attend all grades at your school and not be taught by a teacher of color? A Black teacher?

Your school has made concerted efforts to ensure fairness and equity in the achievement, promotion, and leadership of educators of color.	1 ☐ Not at all	2 ☐ A little	3 ☐ Some	4 ☐ A lot	5 ☐ 100%

- How are the achievements of educators of color recognized and celebrated?
- How are educators of color promoted with full transparency based on merit? How do you provide educators of color with access to influence and decision making at your school? How are they given opportunities to lead and take part in major school decisions?
- How does your school ensure educators of color receive equitable salaries and advancement opportunities to their white colleagues and preclude the imposition of unfair expectations and inequities in responsibilities, support, and evaluation? How do you hold administrators accountable for equitable practices?

Instructional Culture

Your school insists on continual learning, modeling for your students a curiosity to learn new approaches to, as well as perspectives on and interpretations of, all that is taught and how everything is taught.	1 ☐ Not at all	2 ☐ A little	3 ☐ Some	4 ☐ A lot	5 ☐ 100%

- What is taught at your school? Beyond subject matter, what kinds of books, references, or resources are most commonly used?
- To what extent do you ensure different cultural approaches to and interpretations of history and literature as well as mathematics, science, and art?
- How do teachers at your school instruct their students? To what extent do they explore different pedagogical approaches that are consistent with their students' cultures?
- How does your pedagogy ensure equity in resources, including material, technology, and home resources? How do you achieve this equity? What processes have you put into place?

(continued)

FIGURE 3.2 (continued)
School Readiness Tool

You have thoughtfully designed and instituted protocols, procedures, and programs–from hiring to retirement–that encourage educators of color to become great educator-activists whose students excel at your school.	1 ☐ Not at all	2 ☐ A little	3 ☐ Some	4 ☐ A lot	5 ☐ 100%

- How do you (or how will you) ensure educators of color will succeed at your school? How are educators of color supported to become educator-activists?
- How do you welcome and onboard educators of color? How are they respected and cared for? How do you demonstrate that you value the expertise of educators of color?
- How and when do you check in with educators of color to learn about their views on school climate and conditions and their plans for the next school year?
- How do you provide high-quality, meaningful coaching or mentoring support to educators of color? Professional development and fellowship opportunities?

Source: From *Respecting Educator Activists of Color*, by S. El-Mekki, 2020, Center for Black Educator Development.

The eight prompts featured in the figure are part of an incredible tool developed by Sharif El-Mekki of the Center for Black Educator Development (2020) in collaboration with the Pennsylvania Department of Education, Pennsylvania Educator Diversity Consortium, and Mighty Engine. (The entire assessment, which is part of a recruitment toolkit, is cited at the end of this chapter.) Note that the use of the term "educator-activist" in this assessment describes an educator who demonstrates

> a practiced commitment to liberating education from the racism inherent in America's institutions, including our schools, that continue to deny educational equity and prescribe compromised learning and academic outcomes for Black students and, as a result, compromise the humanity of all. (El-Mekki, 2020)

Step 3: Gather Additional Information

Information gathering involves collecting data through surveys, interviews, focus groups, and other techniques for a high-level look at strategies to center the voices of educators of color about school organizational conditions. This delicate matter must be approached with great caution at the risk of racial tokenism, that is, putting additional unpaid burdens on educators of color without intention to act. Listening to educators of color and acting in response to their narratives is a critical factor in workplace satisfaction. All efforts to support and retain educators of color must be guided by these insights, stories, and experiences.

This practice offers multiple benefits:

- Soliciting teacher input through interviews, focus groups, or surveys may shed light on the context undergirding collected data.
- Teacher input may highlight nuances, complexities, or contradictions in quantitative or anecdotal data that cannot otherwise be explained.
- Additional information may reveal issues or problems the instruction leader is unaware of.
- Collecting further information signals leadership's care and concern for teacher well-being.

Focusing on the voices of educators of color is not novel; several seminal studies in school leadership and teacher diversity draw powerful conclusions from the stories and experiences of educators of color. Teach Plus and the Center for Black Educator Development conducted a national study of 105 Black educators across 12 states. Drawing from educator narratives, Mason and team (2021) report five institutional behaviors that positively correlate with retaining educators of color: (1) strategic initiatives prioritize the recruitment, support, and retention of teachers of color; (2) school leadership takes the lead in fostering an inclusive workplace; (3) institutional support exists for culturally responsive and sustaining curricula and teaching practice; (4) the organization provides equity-focused professional learning; and (5) diversity and equity initiatives are embedded in every aspect of school culture. Similarly, Travis Bristol (2018) and Rita Kohli (2018) cite listening to educators of color as a prerequisite to enacting meaningful change in school organizational conditions. Conversely, failure to center the voices of educators of color and address concerns such as low pay, exclusionary discipline, racial hostility, lack of support, and other issues is linked with disengagement and teacher turnover (Stanley, 2021).

Strategies

The term *information gathering* broadly describes techniques used to glean insight from educators of color regarding their lived experiences. Here are some examples of strategies to collect information drawn from leadership, business, and education:

- **Open forums.** Virtual or in-person venues offer a means for educators to engage with each other or with forum facilitators and freely share questions, comments, or insights. The forums, which may be loosely structured, allow for educators to bring up items that concern them with a broader audience.
- **Exit interviews.** Exit interviews provide one-on-one opportunities to gather insight and feedback from employees after they have announced their departure but before they have formally left. Exit interviews typically include predetermined topics or questions focused on workplace experiences, reasons undergirding departure, and future professional aspirations.
- **Stay interviews.** Similar to exit interviews, stay interviews are conducted with individuals who are choosing to stay or as an intervention to encourage retention. Stay interviews may include predetermined topics and questions focused on memorable workplace experiences, challenges, aspirations, goals, and feedback for the organization.
- **Focus groups.** Focus groups are small group sessions comprising 6–10 participants. They are often conducted with preselected topics and questions. Themes may also emerge from participants in the form of new ideas or concerns previously unconsidered.
- **Surveys.** Surveys can be used to solicit written feedback from a predetermined group of people. Questions may be closed-ended (i.e., questions with preset answer choices like true/false or ranked choices) or open-ended (i.e., questions that require a narrative response). Surveys may be anonymous or require self-identification of the survey taker.
- **Pulse meetings.** Whereas exit and stay interviews occur at pivotal times in the school year and are linked to employment decisions to leave or stay at a school, pulse meetings describe any general type of intimate listening session to "check the pulse" of an individual and gather insight about their workplace experiences.

The next sections will take a deeper look into surveys and pulse meetings and the benefits and limitations of these strategies—as well as how these meetings can be structured.

Surveys

The concept of gathering insight through surveys is familiar to many school leaders. Though surveys require intensive planning to develop the appropriate format and questions, many schools use them as part of their modus operandi.

When implemented effectively, surveys can be powerful, but if poorly designed, they produce little feedback. Rather than avoiding surveys, create effective ones by approaching them with intention. First, identify your goals by asking yourself, *What element(s) of my school do I need to learn more about?* Identify who you would like to invite to take the survey and develop a list of questions targeting the areas that you would like to investigate. Then, set up the survey using Google Forms or another platform that allows for quick and easy survey completion and response analysis. Following the collection of survey data, identify initial themes from survey responses for further investigation using pulse meetings.

Surveys may not always bring about expected results. One reason is that surveys are most effective when they accompany regular channels of communication (Laker, 2022). Ongoing surveys that demonstrate a continuous feedback loop often have higher levels of engagement than one-time surveys (Newman, 2016). You may choose to set a consistent and predictable schedule for educators to complete surveys. A word of caution: give yourself enough time to review the data, report results to staff, and respond to feedback raised by making tangible changes. In their study of lack of survey completion among employees, James R. Detert and coresearchers (2010) conclude that employee silence is linked to perceived lack of leadership responsiveness. They argue that many employees do not complete surveys because they perceive they have nothing to gain or lose. In fact, they may consider completing surveys a poor use of limited time because the surveys fail to bring about any change. This raises a critical point: lack of acknowledgement or tangible response to survey findings will adversely impact future efforts to gather meaningful data.

See Figure 3.3 for additional criteria to consider when developing a survey, as well as limitations to keep in mind.

Bearing in mind the multiple demands on educators' time, educators who participate in survey completion should be offered a token of acknowledgment. Compensation as a financial gesture of thanks may be a limitation for some schools and districts. However, it is important to realize that asking for educators to be vulnerable and expend their time and mental capacity to provide feedback is outside the scope of their professional duties. If compensation is not allowed, consider reciprocity—for example, covering a class or portion of a class, giving teachers additional release time, or making another gesture that takes something off teachers' plates.

One-to-One Pulse Meetings

Conducting pulse meetings with teachers is another strategy for gathering information about organizational conditions. Survey results may be telling, but pulse meetings can uncover concerns overlooked or submerged within survey results. However, take care that the onus of improving in-school experiences of educators of color lies with leaders and leadership teams and is not the responsibility of educators of color themselves.

FIGURE 3.3
Considerations for and Limitations of Surveys

Qualities of Effective Surveys	Limitations of Surveys
Topics and questions align with matters that sync with the values, beliefs, and concerns of educators of color	Require extensive planning, especially when developed from scratch
Designed for multimodal facilitation (e.g., online, mobile app, email, paper)	May not lead respondents to provide honest or thorough feedback
Easy to administer and easy to access	May incur survey fatigue or disengagement in respondents
Easy to analyze (survey platforms often include data analysis mode)	Too many questions may result in incomplete response–or none at all
Able to solicit insight and/or feedback from a large group of respondents within a limited amount of time	Respondents may fear retaliation or retribution for providing feedback, even if anonymous
	Respondents may provide inaccurate responses due to misinterpretation of the question or poorly written answer choices

Pulse meetings can take many forms. As with exit and stay interviews, they can focus on predetermined topics and scripted questions. That said, pulse meetings are not the same as stay meetings, which usually gather insight from a staff member to encourage their retention. The intent of pulse meetings is to learn from individual experiences, discerning themes across educators' responses that inspire actionable and sustainable changes to organizational conditions for both individual and collective well-being.

You can schedule pulse meetings with educators in advance or on a predictable, consistent schedule. In addition to quarterly pulse meetings with educators of color, one principal of an urban high school I know implemented a morning coffee hour prior to student arrival to chat with educators and other staff members, who could drop by or sign up for individual slots to build rapport, strengthen connections, discuss educator concerns, or make suggestions. At times, the principal extended individual invitations to solicit feedback about relevant issues facing the staff and faculty. At other times, she invited staff members to a brief meeting to see how they were doing or follow up on recent concerns or feedback they expressed. She also kept notes about her interactions with her staff to ensure their concerns and feedback were not overlooked. In this manner, she made sure to touch base with all her educators, not just the most vocal or expressive ones, to proactively provide support when needed.

Schools and organizations with an embedded structure of weekly or biweekly meetings often confuse the distinction between one-to-one check-ins and pulse meetings. An organizational culture of check-ins often revolves around revisiting schoolwide metrics and professional goals, as well as reviewing previous next steps and planning ahead. These purposes differ from those of pulse meetings. A pulse meeting should center the voice and experiences of educators of color; it is a setting in which leaders explicitly solicit insight about educators' personal and professional aspirations, day-to-day workplace satisfaction, needs, and what steps can be taken to improve the quality of the workplace. They are predicated upon listening—truly listening—for educator insight on how to improve conditions to better support and retain educators of color. As Kim Scott (2020) states in the *Radical Candor* blog about clear, compassionate feedback, "It's also the most important chance for you to hear from your employee, and it's their time, not yours" (para. 21). In short, it is your job to be the lead listener in these meetings. In addition to increasing productivity and engagement, pulse meetings lend themselves to increasing rapport and building empathy, which help mitigate issues of bias and fragmented relationships between leaders and their direct reports.

You can also hold pulse meetings with students of color and their caregivers. As you construct your plan for these meetings, consider how centering these voices will give critical insight into their experiences and may reflect broader themes that also influence teachers of color in your building. If your school does not have any educators of color, reflect on insight from the pulse meetings to uncover underlying reasons for this absence in your building.

Like surveys, pulse meetings are beneficial but may also have some drawbacks. See Figure 3.4 for additional guidance and barriers related to pulse meetings. As you embark on Step 3, consider which strategy or strategies you will use to gather information and devise a tool to do so (e.g., survey, pulse meeting agenda). Then, determine your target audience and estimated timeline for collecting the data. Additional resources are supplied in Appendices B, C, and D to support creating and facilitating pulse meetings. Once you have data in hand, you can move to the next step: analyze findings.

FIGURE 3.4
Considerations for Pulse Meetings

Effective Pulse Meetings	Barriers That Undermine Pulse Meetings
Purpose of meeting and commitment to educator psychological safety and confidentiality established at the beginning of meeting	Absence of rapport or trust may impede truth telling
Guided by an agenda with planned topics and questions of relevance to the interviewee	Lack of leadership credibility may influence the type of information educators divulge
Unattached to mandated one-to-one check-ins (e.g., performance reviews, coaching meetings)	Characterized as a professional task or mandate versus effort to improve workplace conditions
Leader implements active listening and reserves judgment	Failure to validate employee's experiences and opinions
Leader uses probing questions to seek understanding	Facilitator focused on ascertaining gossip or hearsay, not the participant's truth
There is consistent follow-through after the meeting	

Principle 3: Assess and Plan for Action • 61

Step 4: Analyze Findings

Following the processes outlined in this chapter, you have collected a variety of data. These data are a form of evidence; however, the data may be broad and may point to a variety of issues. The tables in Figures 3.5 and 3.6 are designed to facilitate the process of reflecting on data and planning for action. Complete Part A: Reflection Document (Figure 3.5) to reflect on areas of strength. Then, complete Part B: Root Cause Analysis (Figure 3.6) to determine areas of weakness and interrogate potential policies, procedures, and practices that contribute to these areas. Mapping root causes helps determine commonalities across the data, both to share with staff and to guide your action plan.

FIGURE 3.5
Part A: Reflection Document

Strength Areas	Evidence Teacher narratives, quantitative data, etc.	Domains
		• Vision and mission • Leadership culture • Staff dynamics • Instructional culture
		• Vision and mission • Leadership culture • Staff dynamics • Instructional culture
		• Vision and mission • Leadership culture • Staff dynamics • Instructional culture
		• Vision and mission • Leadership culture • Staff dynamics • Instructional culture

FIGURE 3.6
Part B: Root Cause Analysis

Weakness Areas	Evidence *Teacher narratives, quantitative data, etc.*	Potential Root Cause(s) *Policies, procedures, practices*	Domains
			• Vision and mission • Leadership culture • Staff dynamics • Instructional culture
			• Vision and mission • Leadership culture • Staff dynamics • Instructional culture
			• Vision and mission • Leadership culture • Staff dynamics • Instructional culture
			• Vision and mission • Leadership culture • Staff dynamics • Instructional culture

Step 5: Develop Action Plan

Equity work is most effective when it is goal-driven and specific point people are designated to create manageable goals, implement them, and monitor movement toward the desired outcomes. Figure 3.7 walks you through the creation of SMART goals, key tasks, and benchmarks to assess your progress toward your goals.

FIGURE 3.7
SMART Goals, Key Tasks, and Benchmarks

Create SMART Goals

Given the data you have collected, what improvements need to be made to foster a culturally affirming school environment? Create goals related to these improvements that are also in line with broader school priorities.

Examples of SMART Goals

- By March 2024, _____ percent of teachers of color indicate satisfaction with management and feeling valued/respected.
- By June 2024, reduce turnover among staff of color by _____ percent for the upcoming school year.
- By August 2024, increase percentage of ethnic-racial match between teachers and students by _____ percent for the upcoming school year.
- By August 2024, increase ethnic-racial diversity of teacher workforce by hiring underrepresented educators (e.g., individuals identifying as Black, Latino/x, AAPI, American Indian).
- By September 2024, expand capacity by partnering with external organizations to create and implement individualized instructional support plans for 100 percent of educators of color who convey interest.
- By January 2024, _____ percent of teachers indicate "strongly agree" to the question "I am satisfied with the level of support given to me by school leader" on the midyear survey, including satisfaction rate of _____ percent among teachers of color.

Your Turn

1.

2.

3.

4.

(continued)

FIGURE 3.7 (continued)
SMART Goals, Key Tasks, and Benchmarks

Determine Key Tasks

What steps are needed to accomplish your SMART goals? What new policies, procedures, or practices need to be modified—or created from scratch—to meet the desired outcomes? How do these tasks align to the elements of vision and mission, leadership culture, staff dynamics, and instructional culture? How will you embed culturally affirming approaches into each aspect of the tasks? You may find yourself revisiting and redeveloping these tasks. This process of (re)development (i.e., doing it again) is necessary to improve the processes and meet the SMART goals.

Examples of Key Tasks

- (Re)develop onboarding and orientation procedures
- (Re)develop school vision and/or mission statements
- (Re)develop schoolwide symbols and artifacts so they are culturally affirming, respectful, and not racially biased or harmful

- (Re)develop meaningful mentorship opportunities across career stages
- (Re)develop equity-focused training
- (Re)develop affinity groups within/across schools and/or districts

- Implement equitable salary and opportunities for advancement
- (Re)commit to system of recognition, rewards, and workplace flexibility
- (Re)develop systems that center teacher humanity (personal wellness and self-care)

- (Re)develop mechanisms of instructional support, including who provides support, why, and for how long
- (Re)examine curriculum and approaches to teaching to be culturally responsive and center assets of underrepresented communities

Charting Goals and Tasks

Once you have determined your key tasks, connect them with your goals and establish a timeline. An example of what this process might look like follows:

SMART Goals	Key Tasks	Timeline	Domains
Manageable and measurable outcomes to improve elements of culture and working conditions	*Policies, procedures, and practices needed to accomplish the goal(s)*	*Timeline to complete key tasks*	*Element addressed by SMART goals and key tasks*
By June 2024, 100 percent of educators of color indicate satisfaction with individualized instructional support	Develop and facilitate survey that allows educators of color to identify and rank preferred instructional supports for each quarter Review data with broader instructional team Determine owner for each instructional support	August 2023	• Vision and mission • Leadership culture • Staff dynamics • Instructional culture
	Develop eight-week cycles for teacher participation	September 2023	• Vision and mission • Leadership culture • Staff dynamics • Instructional culture
	Develop tool (survey or pulse meetings) to determine teacher satisfaction with support	October 2023	• Vision and mission • Leadership culture • Staff dynamics • Instructional culture

(continued)

FIGURE 3.7 (continued)
SMART Goals, Key Tasks, and Benchmarks

Putting It All Together

Finally, assign an owner for each task and determine methods to monitor progress using the tools presented in this chapter.

SMART Goals	Key Tasks	Timeline	Benchmarks
Manageable and measurable outcomes to improve elements of culture and working conditions	Policies, procedures, and practices needed to accomplish the goal(s)	Timeline to complete key tasks	How change will be monitored, what tools (e.g., surveys, pulse meetings) will be used, who will own each task
By June 2024, 100 percent of educators of color indicate satisfaction with individualized instructional support	Damien to develop and facilitate survey that allows educators of color to identify and rank preferred instructional supports for each quarter Damien to facilitate data review with broader instructional team ALL to determine owner for each instructional support	August 2023	Confirm each teacher completes survey and is placed into at least one of top two preferences for individual instructional support Incorporate morning "chat 'n' chews" with teachers as an open forum to address concerns or questions
	ALL to launch eight-week cycles for teacher participation	September 2023	Incorporate biweekly anonymous surveys using five-point scale (5 = strongly agree, 1 = strongly disagree) to rank satisfaction with support Review data weekly with broader instructional team
	Damien to develop tool (survey or pulse meetings) to determine teacher satisfaction with support over the course of whole support cycle	October 2023	Review data with broader instructional team and use feedback to adjust next round of individualized instructional support cycle

Conclusion

This chapter was designed to provide steps and resources for instructional leaders to assess and plan for action, moving from thinking about educator diversity to developing a concrete and manageable plan for change. We looked to empirical research and teacher voices to consider the foundational elements of organizational conditions that support and retain teachers of color. We explored school vision and mission, leadership culture, staff dynamics, and instructional culture and how these elements function to support—or undermine—workplace satisfaction and educator retention. Next, we examined a five-step plan to collect data and evaluate school readiness to support and retain educators of color. Finally, we followed a step-by-step plan to convert your findings into a plan for action using sample goals, key tasks, and progress benchmarks.

? Reflection Questions

1. In this chapter, we identified school vision and mission, leadership culture, staff dynamics, and instructional culture as integral elements for recruiting and retaining educators of color. Of these elements, which do you find the most compelling and dynamic in your school? Of the four, which element(s) should be prioritized to make your school culturally affirming?
2. Revisit the School Readiness Tool (Figure 3.2) and reread the questions. How does this tool reframe your thinking and vision for your school? What are the implications for instructional leadership? What ideas, questions, or considerations did this assessment raise for you?
3. Reflect on your responses to the School Readiness Tool. How do you think educator(s) of color in your building would respond to the questions? How similar (or different) might your responses be compared with theirs? What if students took the assessment? Students' caregivers and members of the broader school community?
4. Given the data, what do you believe are the strengths of your school? What are areas of weakness? What underlying root causes (e.g., policies, procedures, and/or practice) do you need to target to effect change?

5. Taking steps to make change and foster culturally affirming practices and schools is challenging work; it requires constancy, capacity, and accountability. What will you do to stay committed to this work to better conditions for educators of color?

Beyond the Text: Resources to Level Up

El-Mekki, S. (2020). *Respecting educator activists of color: The anti-racist guide to teacher retention.* Center for Black Educator Development. https://www.thecenterblacked.org/s/CBED21-A2E-Retention-Toolkit-012.pdf

Gruenert, S., & Whitaker, T. (2015). *School culture rewired: How to define, assess, and transform it.* ASCD.

Jackson, R. R. (2021). *Stop leading, start building! Turn your school into a success story with the people and resources you already have.* ASCD.

Kafele, B. K. (2015). *The principal 50: Critical leadership questions for inspiring schoolwide excellence.* ASCD.

Kafele, B. K. (2019). *Is my school a better school because I lead it?* ASCD.

4

PRINCIPLE 4:
Commit to Sustainable and High-Impact Instructional Supports

Our work is our most important resource to develop our people.

—Jim Trinka and Les Wallace

Interviewer: Can you take me through some of your experiences receiving instructional support?

Sasha: I had a manager when I first entered teaching who was impressed by the buy-in that I had with students but thought that I didn't have enough management, so I was coached on management and was encouraged to do things such as having kids cheer in my classroom. A few years later, I had a coach who I thought was phenomenal, but her specialty was not in chemistry, which is frustrating because I am still held accountable to teaching science standards. I found myself asking, "What does it look like in a science classroom?" And honestly, that is the trend that I still find now. A lot of my support has been educators or people who are unable to contribute to my growth as a science teacher. There were years that I didn't really get more support even if I wanted it. I would send out emails and really ask my managers to find support, but it fell on deaf ears.

Sasha's experience is just one instance of disconnect related to instructional support that exists daily in schools all over the nation. While many schools offer structured approaches to guide educator professional growth, it is impact—not intent—that factors into teachers' satisfaction with instructional support.

This chapter focuses on committing to sustainable and high-impact instructional supports for educators of color. This is the chapter you will want to read and reread with pen and highlighter in hand and perhaps even some sticky notes to jot down ideas. Positive perception of instructional support is among the most essential levers for attracting and retaining these educators. We will examine three key areas that instructional leaders can target: pedagogical expertise, professional capacity, and personal well-being. But first, we will dive into the research that frames why instructional support is particularly critical for educators of color.

The Case for Instructional Support

One might argue that effective instructional supports are beneficial for all educators, not just educators of color. Many researchers would likely agree, citing the fact that leadership support of educators accelerates professional growth and is linked with workplace motivation. Sandra Bridwell (2012) reports that availability of instructional supports enhances educator motivation and openness to feedback, which often lead to increased instructional effectiveness. Proactive instructional support is also linked with positive perception of working conditions and educator retention (Brown & Wynn, 2007; Rodgers & Skelton, 2014). While these findings indicate instructional support is valuable to all educators, instructional support is particularly critical for educators of color for three reasons:

- **Many educators of color experience an absence of high-quality support.** Using nationally representative data surveys of K–12 educators, Richard Ingersoll and Robert Connor (2009) report that teachers of color were more likely than white teachers to leave their schools when they lacked support. These trends are particularly salient among early-career educators of color. In their analysis "Why Black Women

Teachers Leave and What Can Be Done About It," Desiree Carver-Thomas and Linda Darling-Hammond (2017b) found that the average early-career educator receives induction and mentoring support to improve teaching. Although Black first-year educators were on par with non-Black early-career educators in receiving these supports, Black educators reported meeting less frequently with mentors than their white counterparts. Black educators were also less likely to report satisfaction with induction and mentoring supports than other early-career educators (11.4 percent compared with 28 percent of all early-career educators). They also found that among early-career educators, Black educators were one tenth as likely as their non-Black peers to receive a full menu of support, including but not limited to common planning time, induction, and mentoring. These data raise questions about equitable access to quality and consistent support to educators of color.

- **Educators of color face disparities in preservice mentorship and clinical experiences.** Many alternative certification programs have become household names in recent decades. Originating as a solution for teacher shortages in hard-to-staff urban schools, these alternative certification programs are popular as cost-effective and accelerated pathways to teaching, particularly for Black teachers and other educator candidates of color who have been historically excluded from wealth-building opportunities and experience disproportionate debt burden, both potential barriers to pursuing postgraduate degrees (Carver-Thomas, 2017). However, these alternative certification programs may provide fewer clinical observations or condensed student teaching experiences under the guidance of an expert instructor. Recent reports indicate that 34 percent of alternative certification graduates are people of color, more than double the percentage of educators of color who have graduated from traditional educator preparation programs (NCES, 2018). In a nationwide analysis, Carver-Thomas and Darling-Hammond (2017b) determined that "nearly half of newly hired Black educators were certified through an alternative pathway compared to just 22 percent of all other first-year educators" (p. 173). Moreover, Black women (who make up over

70 percent of the Black educator workforce) were 3.5 times more likely than other educators to enter the profession without student teaching experience.

While many alternative programs are highly effective, analysis of survey responses by the Center for Teaching Quality revealed significant disparities between graduates from the two pathways to teaching. First, 60 percent of graduates from alternative certification programs rated their classroom management abilities as *good* or *excellent* in comparison with 84 percent of traditional recruits (Berry et al., 2008). Alternative certification program graduates appeared to be less confident in their ability to support struggling students and implement differentiation (38 and 49 percent, respectively) than their counterparts from traditional certification programs (71 and 77 percent).

The education profession has a moral imperative to provide equitable access to educators of color, particularly those who come into schools with less clinical experience than their colleagues. Although some alternative certification programs include several months or up to a year of preservice residency, some educators of color may have had fewer opportunities for hands-on experiences and mentorship. Many excellent educators come from alternative certification programs, but these findings amplify the need for instructional leaders to commit to high-quality, consistent supports for educators of color to maximize their inherent potential and value to the school community.

- **Dissatisfaction with instructional support leads to high turnover.** Although mentioned in Chapter 1, it bears repeating that the perceived shortage of educators of color is exacerbated by a revolving door of educator talent. Richard Ingersoll and his team have investigated factors influencing underrepresentation of educators of color in the teacher workforce over decades and published their findings in numerous manuscripts and reports. In an analysis of national turnover data from 2012–2013 rereleased in 2021, they found that 50 percent of turnover among educators of color was attributed to dissatisfaction, and 81 percent of respondents said that dissatisfaction with leadership actions contributed to their decision to switch schools or leave the profession altogether. Educator turnover is linked with organizational instability, harms staff and student culture, and depletes leadership time and resources better spent on supporting academic achievement.

Many school leaders already see instructional support as a way to further student learning; however, we need to reframe it as a tactic to attract highly talented educators of color, support the development of pedagogical skills and relationship building with students and their families, sustain motivation, and, by extension, retain a highly qualified workforce. Prioritizing sustainable, high-impact support for educators of color communicates their value and integral role in the school community. It says their work is seen and it matters. Yet many educators of color find themselves in Sasha's shoes—longing for instructional support and seeking leadership attention to their professional growth.

Interrogate Lack of Instructional Support

Many of us move into instructional leadership roles with the aspiration to provide the resources that educators need to perform at high levels so that students can be successful. However, these intentions are often overshadowed by other priorities such as budget concerns, staff cuts, and accountability to local, state, and federal mandates. The pivot to remote and hybrid learning models against the backdrop of the COVID-19 global health crisis and overlapping systemic and individual challenges also took a toll on leaders. These challenges continue as many leaders find themselves faced with redesigning systems to address students' and families' postpandemic needs. The work accomplished by school leaders is transformative yet exceedingly hard, and leaders, you deserve credit for all the work you do on the ground for the communities you serve.

In response to competing priorities and demands, instructional leaders and teams often find themselves balancing their own capacity with what is best for the school. They may need to coach educators whose "rooms are on fire" or provide supplemental resources to certain teachers in the months leading up to testing season. Supporting staff with immediate needs may mean that educators who are capable of managing their classrooms and students without requiring attention and feedback are not able to improve their practice in a way that is consistent with their own aspirations. We need to understand the significance of intent versus impact—while school leaders who are spread thin may not intend to withhold support from educators of color, the impact of the circumstances is that the talent, potential, and commitment to student achievement by many educators of color are devalued. The absence of support may be symptomatic of race-based assumptions, stereotypes, or low expectations for students. Guided by Principle 2, *Cultivate reflection and self-awareness,* we need to interrogate why support is lacking and identify levers to enact change. I encourage you to slow down and consider the following teacher voices from the field as you reflect on your own beliefs, experiences, and practice as an instructional leader.

Jay: Race-Based Assumptions

> If you are Black or Brown and you have proven yourself to be able to manage a classroom, the level of support you receive is minimal. There is always an assumption that Black and Brown educators are good classroom managers because many of us can develop strong relationships with kids. Especially as a Black man, I'm constantly being praised for the level of cooperation that I receive from my students. Discipline honestly isn't an issue for me. Gathering from my own experiences and discussions with other educators of color, we aren't developed much past classroom management, so we often have to go to each other for support on how to improve our practice. I came into teaching because I wanted to deliver content in a unique and engaging way to kids. My classroom is considered a model classroom in my school. My white colleagues are constantly asking me for advice about how to work with our students or asking me to conference with their kids. However, it's not about management or disciplining students for me. That's not the goal. The goal is to teach children.

The absence of consistent instructional support can stem from race-based assumptions about educators of color. Many studies explore how Black and Latino/x educators are often assigned to formal and informal disciplinary roles in their schools by their school leaders under the assumption that they are more appropriate to provide behavioral guidance to students due to ethnic, racial, and cultural similarities (Bristol & Mentor, 2018; Brockenbrough, 2015; Carey, 2020; Carter Andrews et al., 2019). However, this approach overlooks their expertise as culturally responsive educators and bridge builders who can develop relationships with students and leverage those relationships to improve academic outcomes. An alternative would be to position educators of color in formal, paid leadership roles to equip colleagues with these skills, enhancing their capability for academic leadership.

Dara: Stereotypes

> Ms. Stevens always danced around the phrase "angry Black woman" in conversation with me. She almost seemed scared or threatened when giving me feedback. She would say, "You know, I don't want to make you mad by giving you this feedback" or "I don't want to make you upset." I think she did this because she knew I was going to ask questions about the feedback. I only did this to get a better idea of how I could improve my teaching for students. But I guess asking questions always made me an "angry Black woman." This made me really miserable, and it felt like she didn't care about my growth at all.

Stereotypes are "a fixed, overgeneralized belief about a particular group or class of people" (Cardwell, 1996). Dara alludes to the stereotype of the "angry Black woman," the misperception of a Black woman's expression of emotions as aggressive or even violent (Jones & Norwood, 2017). Seeking to understand the feedback, she instead encountered demoralizing race- and gender-based stereotypes that undermined her relationship with her instructional leader and inhibited her growth as an educator.

Allan: Low Expectations

> My classroom management was always so tight with my scholars. I was always assigned to work with the lowest level of readers, and I felt like my instructional leader didn't really pay attention to giving me the strategies that I needed to push students along further in their growth. Although my kids were always working, I didn't feel as effective as I wanted to be. I always wanted to be the kind of educator whose instruction alone could drive class engagement—even if my classroom management had an off day! As I reflect, I think classroom management and my relationships with students were the driving forces behind the effort they put in.

When I asked for help, I always had the impression that my leader was satisfied that my room wasn't on fire, my kids were seated and doing their work. But that shouldn't be the bar. It was disappointing.

Inattention to the needs of educators of color may be symbolic of low expectations for children of color and, by extension, educators of color. Allan expresses his disappointment in his quest to develop an instructional skill set that fosters student independence and a love of learning. He sensed a complacency in leaders who set compliance and busywork as the standard for his students to meet, and he found these diminished expectations to be "disappointing."

Committing to Sustainable and High-Impact Supports

The previous sections have made two arguments. First, instructional support is a critical lever that school leaders can use to attract, develop, and retain educators of color. And second, if there are racial inequalities in instructional support, leaders must interrogate the root causes of these disparities. Now it is time to heed the call to action of Principle 4: *Commit to sustainable and high-impact instructional supports,* specifically in three key areas: pedagogical expertise, professional capacity, and personal well-being.

Pedagogical Expertise

Pedagogical expertise is the mastery of content knowledge and teaching strategies used to educate students. After all, teaching is both an art (knowledge and intuition of the process) and a science (ability to convey process and transfer learning). In my experience working in schools nationally and internationally, I often see coaching and professional development that follow the "sit and get" model. Educators are exposed to new information but have limited opportunities for meaningful practice. Early in my career, even I was complicit in the design and facilitation of this type of experience. The "sit and get" model requires substantial time and human resources but offers little return in terms of effects on educator practice. To maximize your limited time and capacity as an instructional leader, consider the following sustainable and high-impact alternatives that have the potential to enhance educators' pedagogical expertise.

Communicate the School's Instructional Priorities

By developing a menu of instructional priorities for the school year, instructional leaders can implement targeted professional development that addresses both content knowledge and teaching strategies. Develop a goal each trimester or quarter that (1) aligns with a trend in educator observations and (2) is rooted in student learning. Provide staff with consistent and regular professional development that targets these priorities and creates meaningful opportunities for them to practice the strategies in their rooms and content areas. You can also implement sequential instructional priorities that build on each other to strengthen educators' skill sets and students' learning. For example, base the instructional priority in the first quarter on setting learning objectives. (Setting clear and specific goals can lead to a gain in student learning of 23 percentile points [Marzano, 2003].) During this time, encourage educators to create planning materials, rigorous exemplars showing objective mastery, or minilessons with their peers. The next quarter, focus on providing meaningful feedback to students based on learning objectives. This progressive approach can enhance educator knowledge of content, facilitate student learning, and provide meaningful opportunities for educators to practice.

Implementation of school instructional priorities also fosters a community of educators-as-learners. Setting instructional priorities establishes a clear vision for teaching, a common language, and opportunities for educators to learn alongside and from each other. If capacity is an issue in the school, you can tap into veteran educators or teams of educators to demonstrate best practices in their classrooms in ways that motivate all educators to develop their pedagogical expertise using hands-on and collaborative practice that translates to their classroom.

Provide Goal-Oriented Observation and Feedback Loops

Another aspect of sustainable and high-impact instructional support is the creation of specific, manageable, realistic goals for educator growth in collaboration with educators themselves. By listening to what educators want and how they desire to grow in their craft, instructional leaders recognize educators as professionals with agency. The key is not to hand down goals and expect your educators to be motivated. Neither is this an invitation to micromanage or to impose additional support on educators who are already satisfied with the status quo. Rather, come up with ideas for goals based on educator and student data but then spend time listening to educators about the areas in which they want to grow. Once goals are set, develop an agreed-upon weekly or biweekly schedule of dates and times for observations and follow-up meetings. This time should be sacred and immovable on your calendar, thereby conveying to the educator how much you value their time and growth. If you are looking to jump-start educator growth, condense the timing between observation and feedback loops so that they occur as often as two to three times a week. Providing multiple observations and feedback aligned to a specific goal increases the number of opportunities for educators to master practice with feedback and guidance.

Instructional leaders have asked me, "Isn't this the same as the evaluations that I am to complete for my team?" The answer is a resounding "No!" Goal-oriented observation and feedback loops are intended to be fully supportive, without the psychological and emotional toll that often accompanies an educator evaluation system. Even in the context of the strongest educator–leader rapport, evaluative observations are often nerve-wracking because of the potentially high stakes related to salary or contract renewal. Goal-oriented observation and feedback loops are therefore most effective as tools for learning that are not linked to defining performance expectations or determining educator job security.

It is important to distinguish between high-impact feedback that moves the needle with educators and feedback that has little effect on educator practice. High-impact feedback incorporates four elements:

- It must be grounded in student outcome data.
- It must draw on instructional and subject matter expertise.
- It must include both positive feedback ("Keep doing this!") and constructive next steps ("Next time, . . . !").
- It must include opportunities for meaningful practice.

Finally, educator growth requires systematic follow-up with feedback. Leaders must intentionally schedule educator observations and follow through consistently. For this practice to work, it must be manageable and sustainable, often taking place the same days and times each week. If scheduling difficulties arise, one way to adapt is to have the educator place a camera in the back of their classroom to record footage and then share it with you.

Facilitate Instructional Rounds

Instructional rounds are another sustainable, high-impact strategy to enhance pedagogical expertise. Instructional rounds are collaborative opportunities for educators to visit their colleagues' classrooms for a targeted observation. Here are some ways to structure this practice:

- Partner with educators to develop an instructional focus for observations using educator and student data, or align instructional rounds with the school's instructional priority.
- Collaborate with educators to develop an observation guide that notes (1) strengths related to instructional focus ("Keep doing this!"), (2) missed classroom opportunities based on student data ("Have you considered . . . ?"), and (3) personal takeaways.
- Create a mechanism for educators to trade their observation guides with their peers within 24 to 48 hours of observation. Another option is to use collaborative planning time for face-to-face conversations and coplanning.

Although educators missing classroom time can be an obstacle, many instructional leaders reap an incredibly high return from well-facilitated instructional rounds. Consider building instructional rounds into common planning time or implementing a buddy swap by having a teacher cover a colleague's class for half a period. Instructional rounds help educators learn from each other, get and give feedback, and incorporate takeaways into their own practice.

Professional Capacity

Professional capacity refers to an educator's ability to perform the necessary out-of-class tasks for student success inside the classroom, such as analyzing student work and progress toward goals, communicating with families, designing differentiated curricula, and monitoring the achievement of individual learners. Professional capacity usually develops with experience; veteran educators often have richly developed job-related know-how. But the most effective instructional leaders do not just wait for educators to acquire this capacity with experience. Instead, they develop systems to equip even the most novice teachers with the knowledge and skills to master the many responsibilities associated with their job.

Schedule Regular Educator Collaboration

One approach to developing professional capacity is to build time into the schedule for grade-level and content-area collaboration with peers, allowing educators to learn from each other. Consider building shared planning time into the bell schedule so that educators can meet at least once a week, either during the school day or after school, when students have left the building. Creating a standard time for grade-level and content-area collaboration allows educators to share best practices or collaborate on job-related responsibilities.

When I was an instructional leader at a midsize urban charter school, teachers had 30 minutes of grade-team collaboration after school in addition to prep time during the school day. When they advocated to have more time to conference with students at the end of the day, we moved the collaboration time to the morning, prior to student arrival. One of the main ways teachers used this time was to work together to identify and monitor progress of at-promise students who exhibited signs of needing additional academic or socioemotional support. During these meetings, educators cocreated support plans for individual students. They also signed up for student mentoring, allowing for each at-promise student to have a point person in the school who could be their advocate and support their improvement. This was an efficient and time-saving strategy; by taking a team approach to interacting with students, contacting parents, and even planning parent meetings, educators were able to support their students more effectively.

Educator collaboration time can be creatively structured in a variety of ways to meet educators' needs and align with the school schedule. For example, if educators are meeting once weekly, consider following a biweekly cycle that allows educators to focus on both student support and problems of practice or educator planning time. This time can be used flexibly, provided there is a coordinated plan based on staff and student needs and buy-in from staff.

Minimize Interferences to Educator Planning Time

Another strategy to build professional capacity is to safeguard educator planning time. I cannot say this enough: it is critical that, as leaders, we provide educator work time and do not interfere with it. Habitual interference conveys to educators that we do not respect their work time and that their labor is subject to the whim of the school. It is particularly critical that educators of color are not assigned unpaid tasks that fall outside their job description, such as translating conversations with families or supporting student discipline. Although the intent may be to leverage the strengths of our educators, we must protect professional boundaries during educators' worktime and lunch so they can focus on the tasks necessary to support student learning. The 30 or 45 minutes spent translating a conversation or de-escalating a student are now an additional 30 to 45 minutes of required work after a long day of teaching, on top of an already long to-do list. While educators may be called on to support their colleagues or assist with tasks around the school, it is critical that we protect the sanctity of educator planning time; to consistently pull educators for unpaid tasks outside the purview of their role can have a detrimental impact.

Personal Well-Being

Instructional leaders must recognize the importance of authentic relationships, care, and concern for educator *personal well-being*. Elise, a third-year Latina educator, gives an example of the effects of these leadership characteristics:

> About three to four years ago, I was in a master's program and attending classes in the evening while working a full-time job as a 3rd grade reading specialist. Due to the workload of my program, there were some days that I only got two or three hours of sleep. One day, my direct manager told me to go home. I was completely thrown off. "Am I improperly dressed

or something?" I asked. She replied, "No, you look very tired. We will find a sub for you today. Go home, rest, and we will see you tomorrow." And just like that, I went home! She never made me feel guilty for taking her up on her offer. She could have easily just bought me a cup of coffee to help me make it through the day. Rather, she understood that in order to be my best self, I need to be healthy and rested. The fact that she cared for me and allowed me to go home on that day meant the world to me.

Ethics of care theory (Noddings, 1995, 2012) identifies care as integral to relationships in school. In an investigation regarding teacher perception of care by leadership, Cornelius van der Vyver and team (2014) found that teachers described leadership actions such as celebrating educator success, maintaining effective discipline policies and high expectations for students, and adhering to the school's vision and mission as indicators of care by school leaders. However, when prompted to evaluate the level of care within the context of interpersonal relationships, "it seems that teachers experienced inadequate psychological care, mainly because principals did not demonstrate a sincere interest in the personal well-being of teachers" (p. 69). In addition, there was a mismatch of principal perception and teachers' experience of care; teachers' ratings of principal care and psychological support were lower than principals' self-ratings. This finding indicates that care is defined by how it is experienced by the cared for, regardless of the intent of the caregiver, which draws us back to the mismatch between intent and impact. To fulfill the intended purpose of supporting well-being, the educator must feel cared for by the leader. This is more than supporting educator self-care; this is radical care (Rivera-McCutchen, 2021), in which culturally affirming leadership practices are upheld by organizational conditions.

Elise clearly felt cared for by her instructional leader. It is also clear that the instructional leader demonstrated care for the educator's well-being and that likely this care surfaced out of her respect and authentic interest in Elise—beyond what she produced in the classroom! I included Elise's story not to suggest that the only way to show care for a teacher's personal well-being is to send them home when they are tired and in need of a break; rather, this anecdote emphasizes the importance of addressing educators' humanity and their holistic health. Here are some nonexamples of how to care for educators' personal well-being:

- Reduce self-care to team building and other types of "forced fun" activities.
- Neglect to solicit educator feedback about organizational conditions and job-related concerns.
- Fail to follow through with educator feedback about organizational conditions and job-related concerns.
- Say "and don't forget self-care" after providing a list of deliverables or tasks.

Alternatively, understand that a sensitivity for educators' personal well-being emerges out of respect for educators and appreciation for their contributions inside and outside the classroom. Care and concern for teachers starts with being visible in classrooms and hallway spaces, engaging with teachers, and showing genuine interest in their lives outside of work. Demonstrations of care can be planned or spontaneous. Attending to staff well-being may require some scheduled activities, such as class coverage, faculty luncheons, tokens of appreciation, and other gestures, but sometimes we have to address educators' needs in the moment, as Elise's leader did, to demonstrate care and concern for their personal well-being.

Conclusion

This chapter highlights Principle 4: *Commit to sustainable and high-impact instructional supports.* Such supports should be provided in three key areas: pedagogical expertise, professional capacity, and personal well-being. Supporting pedagogical expertise involves systematic attention to building educators' content knowledge and expanding their toolkit of teaching strategies. Amplifying educators' professional capacity means equipping them with the time and essential skills to complete the extra tasks often required of 21st century educators. Finally, facilitating educators' personal well-being is critical to communicating to them that they are valued as people and not just workers. Instructional supports in these three areas should be scheduled in leaders' calendars and considered important parts of our daily work. Often, observations go by the wayside in light of a parent visit, or instructional rounds go unplanned because we need to attend to students. However, the data indicate that moment-by-moment, sustainable, high-impact instructional supports make educators of color feel valued and respected as professionals and equip them to be the best educators they can be.

? Reflection Questions

1. Consider the current instructional support systems at your school. Are supports allocated equitably for all educators? If not, what barriers interfere with sustainable and high-impact instructional supports?
2. Reflect on the voices from the field included in this chapter. What safeguards can be put in place to ensure that decisions regarding instructional support are not influenced by race-based assumptions, stereotypes, or low expectations?
3. Consider your work schedule and weekly rhythms. How do you safeguard time for planning and implementation of instructional support? How do you safeguard classroom observations and feedback meetings? How might you strengthen your professional boundaries to expand your capacity for sustainable and high-impact instructional supports?
4. Consider the three support areas: pedagogical expertise, professional capacity, and personal well-being. Which of the three areas do you perceive is most robustly addressed in your school? How can you partner with other leaders and educators to ensure this area remains a sustainable aspect of your instructional culture and yields a high impact?
5. Of the three support areas, which is an area of growth for your school? What is one step you can take tomorrow to improve in that area?

Beyond the Text: Resources to Level Up

Pedagogical Expertise

Kafele, B. K. (2016). *The teacher 50: Critical questions for inspiring classroom excellence.* ASCD.

Rodman, A. (2019). *Personalized professional learning: A job-embedded pathway for elevating teacher voice.* ASCD.

Professional Capacity

Edwards, J. (2014). *Time to teach: How do I get organized and work smarter?* ASCD.

Heyck-Merlin, M. (2012). *The together teacher: Plan ahead, get organized, and save time!* Jossey-Bass.

Scherer, M. (Ed.). (1999). *A better beginning: Supporting and mentoring new teachers.* ASCD.

Personal Well-Being

Benson, J. (2017, December 1). When teacher self-care is not enough. *Educational Leadership, 75*(4). https://www.ascd.org/el/articles/when-teacher-self-care-is-not-enough

Johnson, M. M. (2022, July 11). Self-care is not enough! *Educational Leadership, 79*(9). https://www.ascd.org/el/articles/self-care-is-not-enough

5

PRINCIPLE 5:
Foster Supportive Environments for Culturally Responsive Approaches

Cultural differences should not separate us from each other, but rather cultural diversity brings a collective strength that can benefit all of humanity.

—Robert Alan

Culturally responsive teaching [is] an educator's ability to recognize students' cultural displays of learning and meaning making and respond positively and constructively with teaching moves that use cultural knowledge as a scaffold to connect what the student knows to new concepts and content in order to promote effective information processing. All the while, the educator understands the importance of being in a relationship and having a social-emotional connection to the student in order to create a safe space for learning.

—Zaretta Lynn Hammond

Interviewer: If you could change one thing about your work as a classroom teacher, what would it be?

Danielle: I would definitely change the expectations around the curriculum and the content I am asked to teach. Students deserve to have a worldwide perspective, especially when it comes to English language arts, history, science, and the other subjects I teach! They deserve to understand the truth about themselves and other people. The world is so much more multidimensional than it's portrayed in our textbooks, but I am limited in how I can respond in my classroom. If my students had a broader understanding about themselves and others, it would allow them in return to get a better idea of how to interact with people who are of different backgrounds and cultures other than their own.

As we enter our school each day, each of us brings a bag—a satchel, a purse, a messenger bag—packed with the necessary supplies to accomplish our practice. We also each bring a "cultural backpack" to school. These backpacks bear our intersecting markers of identity, worldviews, languages, stories, and forms of expression—all of which make ethnic-racial and cultural diversity beneficial to the school community! Likewise, our students bring their own backpacks, filled with identities drawn from varied local and global communities, that are assets to learning.

This backpack metaphor undergirds one of many reasons to diversify the educator workforce. Guided by their own intersecting identities and lived experiences, many educators of color have a unique sensitivity to understanding the cultural backpacks of their students and designing instruction that is relevant to the students' everyday lives. This insight into cultural backgrounds and translation to classroom practice are referred to as *culturally responsive approaches* to education. Multiple studies indicate culturally responsive approaches have a pronounced positive effect on academic achievement and educational experiences for all students, regardless of race, ethnicity, nationality, skin color, gender identity, sexuality, language, ability, and social class, among other identity markers (Aronson & Laughter, 2016, 2020; Ladson-Billings, 1994, 1995).

Despite the benefits associated with culturally responsive approaches, educators of color often find curriculum fails to honor or reflect the diverse cultural backgrounds of their students and their communities of origin. They also often experience barriers that complicate their ability to integrate culturally responsive approaches into their practice. Thus, the need for Principle 5: *Foster supportive environments for culturally responsive approaches.* Culturally affirming instructional leadership practices must include deliberate efforts to ensure educators of color are trusted, equipped, and supported in their implementation of culturally responsive approaches. Instructional leaders must also intentionally create and nurture organizational conditions that are antiracist at their core and welcome diverse representation, forms of cultural knowledge, perspectives, and traditions. But before we delve into strategies for instructional leaders, we will examine the characteristics of culturally responsive approaches, their benefits, and why they matter.

> **A Note About Culture**
>
> Because the term *culture* will be used extensively in this chapter, it is important to come to a consensus on its meaning. The definition of culture is elusive and ever-evolving (Krasilnikova & Sevastyanova, 2015; Robertson, 1988), but the concept can be understood as the characteristics or way of life for a group of people based on demographic factors (including but not limited to ethnicity/race), geographic region, or a combination of factors (Steensland, 2011). Culture is often conceptualized in terms of language, music, customs, dress, folklore, food, and even religion. These are merely overt markers of culture, however; below the surface, culture also comprises social behaviors, values, and beliefs about self and others (Sorokin, 1947). For example, one child's cultural backpack may espouse particular attitudes about justice, personal space, or even self-advocacy, whereas a child from a different cultural background may hold very different views on these topics. What is below the surface is often even more important than what is on the surface.
>
> To avoid stereotype-laden assumptions or deficit beliefs, it is critical for all educators to position themselves to learn about their students' cultural backgrounds and form relationships with both students and their caregivers.

Culturally Responsive Approaches Explored

Camika: I teach so many beautiful children from all over the world. In a world of mic pulling, muting, and silencing, I feel like I have a duty to my babies as a Black woman. I want them to keep their culture alive inside of them. I want them to know their culture is important, so that they don't feel ashamed of it. I want them to feel welcome and know it's okay to speak their Spanish, their Khmer, or their Portuguese, or whatever language they want in front of their teacher, and it's okay and it's an asset to our learning. I think it's those little things that can change the world for these babies.

The labeling and technical use of culturally responsive approaches emerged into the public spotlight during the 1960s and 1970s amid desegregation mandates that exposed school policymakers and educators alike to growing cultural divides in the classroom and ethnic-racial imparity between educators and students (Aronson & Laughter, 2016). However, some maintain that the characteristics associated with culturally responsive approaches are consistent with historical depictions of teaching practices implemented by educators of color, who "bring a unique angle of vision to their work" (Dixson & Dingus, 2008, p. 805). In other words, some argue that cultural responsiveness has always been embedded in the work of educators of color to "validate the struggles, challenges, and celebrations" of their minoritized students and enact a shared vision of educational access and opportunity in partnership with the local community (Mason et al., 2021, p. 10). For instance, in his analysis of Reconstruction and Jim Crow–era schools in the South, Adam Fairclough (2004) argues that Black teachers' firsthand experiences, connections to students' families, and knowledge of students' cultural practices equipped them to effectively instill a love of learning and self-determination in their students despite lack of resources and funding. Findings by James Anderson (1988), Michele Foster (1993, 1995), and Jarvis Givens (2021) convey that as early as the 18th century, Black teachers implemented approaches that honored their students' backgrounds while also seeing the classroom as a site of empowerment and sociopolitical change. Similar studies investigating Latino/x, Native Hawaiian, Asian, and Native American educators' use of students' indigenous language(s), communication patterns, and other cultural practices also identify the ways educators of color draw upon students' cultural backgrounds and knowledge to bridge gaps between home and school (Au, 1980; García-Nevarez et al., 2005; Mohatt & Erickson, 1981; see also Villegas & Irvine, 2010).

Two Models: Examining Culturally Responsive Teaching and Culturally Relevant Pedagogy

A good starting point for understanding culturally responsive approaches is to examine the features of well-known models. The culturally responsive teaching model originated from the work of Geneva Gay (2002). This approach focuses on curriculum and instruction as levers to empower students academically, relay high expectations, integrate students' cultural background and knowledge into curricula, build upon students' assets, and address the needs of the whole child. Social justice also underpins Gay's work. She writes that practitioners of culturally responsive teaching disrupt deficit notions about underrepresented communities and validate cultural forms of knowledge and backgrounds by lifting "the veil of presumed absolute authority from conceptions of scholarly truth typically taught in schools" (Gay, 2010, p. 38; see also Aronson & Laughter, 2016).

Introduced by Gloria Ladson-Billings (1995), the culturally relevant pedagogy model is a paradigm that "empowers students intellectually, socially, emotionally, and politically using cultural referents to impart knowledge, skills, and attitudes" (pp. 16–17). Ladson-Billings uses her observations to note effective teaching strategies, such as drawing connections from students' prior knowledge and everyday experiences to the classroom; fostering collaboration and mutual interdependence among students; instilling sociopolitical awareness to identify, explain, and act against injustice; problematizing curriculum; and developing skills to navigate and overcome inequality. Like those who engage in culturally responsive teaching, educators who employ culturally relevant pedagogy are influenced by their own critical awareness of their intersecting identities and the broader historical and political context of their school and society.

Shared Characteristics of Culturally Responsive Approaches

This chapter uses *culturally responsive approaches* as an umbrella term to signify the traits the seminal models described have in common. Ana María Villegas and Tamara Lucas (2002) theorize that these approaches are neither prescriptive nor identical. However, they do share the following characteristics:

- They create student-centered opportunities to develop academic skills and conceptual thinking.
- They foster critical reflection on self, others, and community.
- They center curriculum that imparts asset-based representation of diverse cultural backgrounds in which students see and appreciate their and others' distinctiveness.
- They engage students in critical and challenging discourses about power, inequality, and strategies to collectively advance justice, both within and beyond the school walls.

In recent years, other models have emerged, including but not limited to culturally sustaining pedagogy (Paris & Alim, 2014), antibias and antiracist teaching (Ramirez & Donovan, 2021), abolitionist teaching (Love, 2019), and historically and culturally responsive frameworks (Muhammad, 2020). These models bear important distinctions, but they do overlap with the models and characteristics of culturally responsive approaches outlined in this section.

Culturally Responsive Approaches Matter

Sylvia: I have a Muslim student in my class from Pakistan. A lot of the other students had questions, so I decided to read the book *Mommy's Khimar*. It was like a light coming on for her and for the other kids in class. After circle time, she came up to me with a glowing face and a grin from ear to ear. I could tell she felt included—I could tell that she felt the love, to be seen in that way. As long as they are happy and learning, that is what is most important to me.

Culturally responsive approaches have been found to positively influence students' educational experiences (Aronson & Laughter, 2016; Villegas & Lucas, 2002). Specifically, these approaches establish a learning environment with the following benefits:

- Trust, solidarity, and familial bonds are nurtured between culturally competent educators and students due to shared knowledge.

- Home and community cultural practices and languages are valued as strengths and springboards for teaching and learning instead of perceived as deficiencies or irrelevant.
- Students are treated with dignity and regarded as competent and deserving intellectuals that matter in the classroom and in society.
- Teaching and learning are structured to foster positive identity development, pride in one's cultural background and intersectional identities, and appreciation for other ways of life.
- Deficit-oriented, biased, stereotypical, or merely inaccurate portrayals of historically underrepresented communities are replaced with asset-based representations.
- Students are treated as agents in their own learning, thus creating a safe space for courageous conversation and critical reflection on their own lives and society.
- Intellectual and psychological safety is emphasized through promoting collaboration, respectful interactions, and elimination of judgment within and across the lines of difference.
- Students have access to multiple and differentiated opportunities to acquire, display, and advance knowledge.
- Students' caregivers and communities of origin are respected as valuable partners in students' educational experiences and have a positive influence.

Culturally responsive approaches appear to relate positively to student learning and academic achievement, resulting in higher graduation rates (Duncan-Andrade, 2007), decreased absenteeism (Wortham & Contreras, 2002), and higher academic achievement in comparison with peers who did not receive culturally responsive instruction (Choi, 2013). Findings by Jacque Ensign (2003) and Tarcia Hubert (2014) reveal students who experienced culturally responsive curriculum and instruction reflected positively on learning experiences, increased time on task, and raised their academic standing from pre- to post-test assessments. Yvonne Bui and Yvette Fagan (2013) also report a schoolwide increase in student reading levels when there was an institutional commitment to culturally responsive approaches among teaching staff. To this end, culturally responsive approaches matter and are significant for all learners.

Significance of Absence

Prudence: I make it a point to integrate my students' backgrounds and identities into the classroom. Science ain't [only] Thomas Edison! Who do you think created the traffic light? A Black man! Did you iron your clothes for school this morning? Who do you think redesigned the modern ironing board as we know it? Black woman. Traffic light? Home security system? Mop? Toilet? Ice cream scooper? Black people! Don't just think that only Europeans were inventors because that's all your books teach you. We unpack these things in my class because it's important students know about the contributions made by those within their community.

Jean: All my kids are Black and Brown. . . . There is no way I will be complicit in whitewashing them.

Instructional leaders who successfully support and retain teachers of color know that culturally responsive approaches go far beyond "heroes and holidays" or "food, festivals, and fun" (Gorski, 2012, p. 398). Instead, they embed cultural responsiveness into the fabric of the school and make it the cornerstone of teaching and learning. As Prudence and Jean convey, culturally responsive approaches matter to educators of color who wish for their students' identities and backgrounds to be reflected and honored in the classroom. To this end, instructional leaders' efforts to foster supportive environments for educators of color and their pedagogies must have deep-rooted clarity about why culturally responsive approaches matter and the implications of the absence of such approaches. In other words, instructional leaders must consider cultural responsiveness as a *need to have* component of their instructional culture, not a *nice to have* one. This commitment to cultural responsiveness must be accompanied by two key understandings: (1) absence of culturally responsive approaches reinforces systemic miseducation, and (2) absence of culturally responsive approaches perpetuates institutional colorblindness.

Absence of Culturally Responsive Approaches Reinforces Systemic Miseducation

A commonly held misconception is that curriculum is *cultureless* if culturally responsive approaches are absent. These assumptions are undergirded by the ill-conceived premise that schools themselves are neutral and impartial to race, creed, or color. This is a baseless assumption. It fails to take into account the past and present ways education policy and practice have actively reified oppression, discrimination, and prejudice, particularly among students and communities of color. In fact, according to scholars, curriculum was often the vehicle by which these harms were inflicted. For example, some textbooks have perpetuated historical myths by using terms like "African immigrants" and "workers" instead of truthfully discussing en masse displacement and chattel slavery. The assets and contributions of communities of color both in the United States and abroad have been rendered invisible in science, math, and other disciplines, while the roles of Europeans are often hypervisible. The realities of genocide, stolen land, and concentration camps have been erased or muted. Even the American literary canon skews heavily toward Western male influence and fails to reflect the rich representation of diverse writers, poets, and folklorists. Such omissions and distortions in curriculum reflect what Lisa Delpit (1988) refers to as the "power of the publishers of textbooks and developers of the curriculum to determine the view of the world presented" (p. 283), thus manifesting an imbalanced understanding of society.

The absence of culturally responsive approaches is problematic for all children, not just children of color. Antiracist activist and scholar Peggy McIntosh (1990) reflected on her miseducation in school and how it contributed to her worldview as a white woman:

> My schooling gave me no training in seeing myself as an oppressor, as an unfairly advantaged person, or as a participant in a damaged culture. I was taught to see myself as an individual whose moral state depended on her individual moral will. (p. 1)

In *White Privilege: Unpacking the Invisible Knapsack*, McIntosh provides concrete examples of how her miseducation was propagated through imbalanced, Eurocentric representation in school curricula. She explains, "When I am told about [American] national heritage or about 'civilization,' I am shown that people of my color made it what it is" (p. 1). She notes the role of curriculum in maintaining her ignorance of global cultures, saying, "I can remain oblivious of the language and customs of persons of color who constitute the world's majority without feeling in my culture any penalty for such oblivion" (p. 1). In this manner, McIntosh illustrates how omitted or distorted representations in curriculum shaped her miseducation about herself and the communities of color that constitute the global majority (Tatum, 2017).

Absence of Culturally Responsive Approaches Perpetuates Institutional Colorblindness

Gholdy Muhammad (2020) explains that colorblindness is harmful to students and their learning: "When educators say they don't see race, they are expecting students to conform to a skills-only curriculum and whiteness. Beyond race, they are also choosing to not see students' cultures, genders, religions, or their magic, while not honoring Black and Brown brilliance in teaching practices" (quoted in Ferlazzo, 2019, para. 31). As such, colorblindness moderated through curriculum and instruction fails to acknowledge and affirm students' rich backgrounds, cultural practices, and embodied knowledge from their communities. In particular, the absence of culturally responsive approaches eliminates the possibility of students of color resonating with the curriculum through positive representations of their everyday experiences and their relevance to school and learning (Love, 2019). Instead, all too often, students are exposed to the following:

- Curriculum that reinforces prejudice, stereotyping, or generalization on the basis of identity through misrepresentation or erasure (e.g., a shortage of picture books featuring dark-skinned children or positive representations of different hair textures) (Guilfoyle, 2015).
- Pedagogy that misappropriates and mocks communities of color. One such example is in the 2021 video reported by NBC News and other media outlets of a white teacher mimicking Native American dancing while wearing a makeshift headdress during a classroom lesson on SOHCAHTOA, a mnemonic device related to trigonometry functions.
- Learning activities that are dehumanizing and reinforce that students of color do not matter, such as racist mock slave auction lessons in which Black children are asked to participate as enslaved people (Cole, 2019).
- Demeaning classroom conditions imbued with discriminatory language and racial epithets. Numerous examples have been observed in multiple

viral videos between 2020 and 2021 in which white teachers in Oklahoma, Maryland, Florida, and North Carolina refer to Black students with the N-word (Cavazos, 2021; Rogo, 2020; Slisco, 2021).

Culturally responsive approaches accomplish more than just addressing racial wrongs committed by a few bad apples or biased curriculum writers. They also signal an institutional commitment to uproot intersectional inequalities and foster welcoming environments where all students have access to equitable, high-quality learning opportunities in which they see themselves and others rightly regardless of race, ethnicity, nationality, skin color, gender identity, sexuality, language, ability, and social class, among other factors.

Barriers to Culturally Responsive Approaches

Jamie: In my school, everything is geared toward what will help students improve their standardized test [scores]. I often feel micromanaged to teach in one way, and my lesson plans are constantly scrutinized to ensure I narrowly focus on test preparation materials. It feels like every day is a formal observation. If the tasks I give kids don't look exactly like the state test, I feel like I'm looked at as a bad teacher.

By now, the significance of culturally responsive approaches and their benefits for students should be clear. However, a paradox remains: studies show that educators of color—and by extension, educators more broadly—face multiple barriers that complicate or undermine their attempts to employ these approaches.

Barrier 1: Misunderstandings About Culturally Responsive Approaches

Brittany Aronson and Judson Laughter (2016) explain that culturally responsive approaches have always faced resistance due to a misunderstanding of their characteristics and what they look like in the classroom. Culturally responsive approaches are neither prescriptive nor invariable. As such, they can blend in seamlessly with a wide range of instructional approaches. For example, Ladson-Billings (1994) observed three teachers using different instructional styles (from teacher-dominant to student-centered). Despite the teachers' seemingly incongruent ways of teaching, she reports common classroom characteristics, including intellectually rigorous instruction, trusting relationships, high expectations, individualized support, and meaningful classroom activities that related to students' everyday lives. In other words, culturally responsive approaches are "good teaching" that can be integrated across different instructional styles.

Culturally responsive approaches are often misperceived as incompatible with standards-driven teaching, an instructional fad, or only for students of color. Empirical evidence shows otherwise. Analyses of qualitative and quantitative studies find that culturally responsive approaches in the classroom deepen acquisition of content and grade-level standards (Aguirre & Zavala, 2013; Civil & Khan, 2001; Langlie, 2008; Rodriguez et al., 2004). Additional studies focused on English language learners illustrate that students of different linguistic backgrounds also benefit from these approaches (Choi, 2013; Wortham & Contreras, 2002), as do white students. Swalwell (2012) explores the effects of culturally responsive education in a predominantly white, affluent suburb. Students who had previously failed to recognize their class and racial privilege extended their thinking by examining how housing policies, racism, and suburbanization helped to explain differences between their community and urban city centers. This culturally responsive activity supported white students in broadening their horizons with respect to contemporary social issues and intersecting inequalities.

Barrier 2: Standardization

Another barrier to implementing culturally responsive approaches is the increasing focus on standardizing education through high-stakes testing and scripted curricula. Influenced in part by education policy such as the No Child Left Behind Act, supporters often rationalize the rise in standardization as a reform tactic to remedy underperformance (Lipman, 2011). However, standardization is also linked with deprofessionalizing the teacher workforce, high accountability, and shrinking autonomy (Achinstein & Ogawa, 2012; Lees et al., 2021; Milner, 2013; Rubin, 2011). These negative outcomes are particularly salient among educators of color, who constitute a higher percentage of the teaching workforce in low-income schools

(Schaeffer, 2021). Findings by Richard Ingersoll (2009) and Betty Achinstein and Rodney Ogawa (2012) indicate teachers in standardized contexts often feel disempowered. Despite a desire to connect students' cultural backgrounds, knowledge, and practices with their learning, teachers are often discouraged from thinking "outside the box." Often, their usage of the curriculum and classroom are highly surveilled and scrutinized. Although some educators of color say they are not held to these expectations because they do not teach a tested subject, findings by Amber Pabon (2016) show that leadership oversight and heightened accountability for educators of color discourages creativity, erodes workplace satisfaction, and undermines the appeal that drew them to teaching in the first place.

Barrier 3: Leadership Assumptions

Instructional leaders must tread carefully with their assumptions about educators' skill and will related to culturally responsive approaches. For example, it cannot be assumed that any educator, even an educator of color, is culturally competent. Cultural competence is not an inherited trait. Educators of color may share ethnic-racial similarities with students but have different cultural experiences due to family origins, socioeconomic class, or other dimensions of their identity. Inadequate support in the areas of cultural competence and culturally responsive approaches can lead to educators of color feeling isolated and ill equipped to meet their professional goals and support their students.

Culturally responsive approaches must also be disentangled from assumptions that educators of color "save" students of color or are solely responsive for improving their academic and educational outcomes. These assumptions place undue burden on educators of color and complicate how they perceive their use of culturally responsive approaches (Achinstein & Ogawa, 2012). Educators of color may feel as if they are being asked to represent, explain, or advocate for their community, positioning them as racialized tokens.

These misguided assumptions reflect two problematic ideologies, the first being the view that students of color, particularly those in economically disadvantaged communities and low-performing schools, lack agency and social support. Students are portrayed as in need of "rescuing" by educator-benefactors from their families and communities of origin, who are often assumed to be complicit in students' underachievement. The second problematic ideology is the presumption that educators can solve the problem of the so-called "achievement gap" without addressing underlying inequalities (e.g., school funding disparities) that have led to widening opportunity differences between students of color and their white and wealthier peers.

Principle 5: Foster Supportive Environments for Culturally Responsive Approaches

Yesenia: In my last school, the emphasis was that our English language learners only spoke English and not their native language. It got to the point that even I started forgetting my Spanish. But in my new school, the teacher coaches and principals encourage connecting with the students in their native tongues and incorporating relevant examples in our lessons. Just last week, we read a biography about Sonia Sotomayor and another great book that had text in Spanish and in English that my colleague lent to me. It makes me look forward to coming to school every day, knowing that my students' diverse backgrounds are valued. It helps me to also feel valued and reconnect with my roots! Even my non-Spanish speakers have started speaking Spanish.

We have established that culturally responsive approaches hold multiple benefits for all students, but although educators of color are drawn to these techniques, they often encounter barriers to their implementation. Educators of color are set up to thrive when these barriers are intentionally uprooted by culturally responsive leaders who are attentive to intersectional diversity, representation, and the cultural attributes of students they serve and their communities (Khalifa et al., 2016). In other words, instructional leaders must first commit to culturally responsive behaviors as an aspect of their leadership so they can foster environments amenable to these approaches. The next section examines strategies in three categories: (1) curriculum and instruction, (2) teacher capacity and resources, and (3) community partnerships.

Curriculum and Instruction

Instructional leaders can begin the process of fostering supportive environments for culturally responsive approaches by closely examining the school's instructional culture and expectations surrounding curriculum and instruction. Specifically, instructional leaders foster supportive environments by making two strategic moves: (1) enhance teacher autonomy and (2) center identity and criticality.

Enhance Teacher Autonomy

Instructional leaders need to consider the ways curricula, as well as expectations for teaching and learning, create (or limit) opportunities for educators of color to effectively implement culturally responsive approaches, which require flexibility to adapt and modify materials to meet the needs of students and pivot as needed to respond to in-school or out-of-school events that influence how students interact with each other, the school environment, and the world. Here are practical ways to enhance autonomy for educators of color:

- **Value their expertise.** Validate the preservice training and professional experiences that educators of color bring to the table. Understand that their proximity to students, personal backgrounds, and skills grant them unique insight to positively influence their students.
- **Set baseline parameters.** Create and convey clear expectations for instructional nonnegotiables in the classroom, including empirically based best practices (e.g., setting learning goals, multiple rounds of student-centered practice) that hold space for educator creativity and responsiveness to students' needs.
- **Humanize classroom monitoring practices.** The ways educators of color experience evaluation, observation, and feedback implicitly set the tone for the type of autonomy they have as professionals to adjust their practice to meet students' needs. The perception of being surveilled may limit educators' comfort with changing their approach to meet student needs. Teaching is both an art and a science, and culturally responsive approaches, like other pedagogical techniques, take time and practice to refine. Educators of color need to feel safe to apply new

techniques, incorporate new activities, and challenge their students in ways that are meaningful to them. This feeling of safety is of particular importance when voices of individuals from underrepresented or economically disadvantaged backgrounds are often systematically silenced in dialogues about educating children of their own communities (Delpit, 1988).

Center Identity and Criticality

Instructional leaders must evaluate the extent to which their curriculum explores issues of identity (including race, ethnicity, nationality, skin color, gender identity, sexuality, language, ability, and social class). The curriculum must also be assessed in terms of positive representation and inclusion of counterstories of historically marginalized and minoritized groups. Positive representation reframes diversity in ways that interrupt stereotypes and caricatures, fostering positive identity development and pride in one's authentic self as well as an appreciation for other communities. On the other hand, counterstories challenge widely held assumptions and bring forward previously overlooked perspectives. One example is using primary and secondary source material centering the voices and viewpoints of Native Americans in a social studies class to understand history through their eyes instead of from the colonizer's perspective. The use of counterstories may uncover themes of resistance, resilience, and culture instead of focusing only on stories of oppression and disenfranchisement.

One helpful tool is the Culturally Responsive Curriculum scorecard, an evidence-based instrument produced by the Education Justice Research and Organizing Collaborative in collaboration with New York University's Steinhardt School of Education. The scorecard draws on themes such as author diversity, representation, and centering students' assets as criteria for assessing curricular and instructional materials.

Cultural responsiveness also requires a focus on criticality, which Gholdy Muhammad (2020) defines as twofold. The first part involves students taking on the intellectual work of a lesson through active reading, writing, thinking, and speaking, and listening. The second part is the use of lessons that connect learning to issues of everyday social relevance by interrogating concepts of power, oppression, and social change. Some curricula may not be predisposed to engaging with identity and criticality due to author or publisher bias, leading back to the need for curricula to be conducive to adaptation as well as the importance of teacher autonomy to modify instruction to meet students' needs.

In her commentary on centering identity and criticality, Gholdy Muhammad (Ferlazzo, 2020; see also Muhammad, 2020) provides excellent reflection questions for instructional leaders on how these tenets show up in curriculum and instruction (amended here to fit our purposes).

- Does the curriculum have the potential to advance students' sense making of their multiple identities and the identities of others? What will students learn about themselves?
- Does the curriculum have the potential to advance students' criticality? What opportunities will students have to think about power, privilege (entitlement), and oppression in the text, in communities, and in society?

Teacher Capacity and Resources

Instructional leaders can also foster a supportive environment for culturally responsive approaches by boosting capacity in educators of color and providing resources to implement these approaches in their classrooms. Two strategies can help with this endeavor: (1) structure reflection and learning, and (2) prioritize teacher planning and collaboration.

Structure Reflection and Learning

Implementation of culturally responsive approaches cannot be divorced from educators' awareness of their own intersectional identities, their relationships to power and privilege, and the social context in which they exist. Educators of color may be aware of some of their most salient identities (e.g., race, gender) while overlooking others that may be more subtle (e.g., ability, gender expression). Instructional leaders can structure opportunities for all educators to reflect and learn about their own blind spots and personal biases related to other identity markers and communities. This process of reflection and learning in turn facilitates educators' proficiency at navigating cultural differences in the classroom. We will look at additional strategies to support reflection and learning in Chapter 6.

Helpful strategies to support educators of color in their reflection and learning include instituting schoolwide book clubs or targeted professional development, but in my work, I find that many leaders who would love to engage in this work lack the time or personal capacity to take on planning these experiences. One solution is to partner with institutions of higher education or external providers to increase capacity and resources for this type of support. Instructional leaders can also offer their educators independent opportunities to reflect on the intersection between identity and classroom practices. Learning for Justice has self-guided cultural competency modules that provide a good jumping-off point, and many national and local conferences may also be appropriate, including the following:

- White Privilege Conference
- Coalition of Schools Educating Boys of Color
- National Association for Multicultural Education
- People of Color Conference
- Teachers 4 Social Justice
- National Association of Independent Schools

Prioritize Teacher Planning and Collaboration

Fostering supportive environments for culturally responsive approaches also requires leadership commitment to teacher planning and collaboration. This practice is of critical importance for all educators, not least those who endeavor to adopt culturally responsive approaches. Instructional leaders can safeguard teacher planning time, both independent and collaborative. They can encourage idea and resource sharing to connect daily instruction to students' everyday lives and backgrounds. To support collegial planning and collaboration, one network implemented a shared Google Drive, with folders related to content-specific topics, for teachers to pool lesson plans, resource links, classroom videos, and soft copy materials for easy access. Even new teachers could take advantage of these materials. It was a great example of thinking (and acting) outside of the box to help every educator implement culturally responsive approaches.

Effective teacher planning time and collaboration also requires trust and feelings of psychological safety. One effective approach is the critical friends model: mutually dependent, collegial, and constructive partners, in dyads or triads, who engage in reflection, learning, and instructional planning. Similar to instructional rounds (see Chapter 4), the critical friends strategy relies on colleagues to prompt each other to consider how issues of bias and cultural responsiveness influence their classroom practices by reviewing assignments, observing instruction, contributing feedback, discussing strengths and challenges of teaching, and providing mutual accountability related to mindset and beliefs regarding students and their networks.

Community Partnerships

The intentional coordination of community partnerships among educators, students, and their networks is of critical importance to families of color and economically disadvantaged communities, who are often overlooked as knowledgeable agents who care for and can contribute to learners' education. By extending opportunities for collaboration both within and outside school, instructional leaders model cultural responsiveness and act in solidarity with educators of color to bridge gaps between home, school, and the broader community. Instructional leaders can implement two strategies: facilitate routine home–school–community collaboration, and manage input and collective decision making.

Facilitate Home-School-Community Collaboration

Educators of color most often bear the burden of becoming cultural translators, interpreters, and bridges between their students and schools (Villegas & Irvine, 2010). Instructional leaders can support their educators of color, students, and broader communities by facilitating meaningful collaboration with these groups and valuing them as invested partners in learners' educational journeys. This collaboration must extend beyond Parent–Teacher Night or report card conferences to include providing school-based resources and personnel to facilitate engagement opportunities, relationship building, and other endeavors that center the needs, aspirations, histories, cultures, and traditions of students and their contexts. Home–school–community collaboration also furnishes insight into the assets of diverse students and the ways their cultural backgrounds, traditions, and languages can be tapped to further learning.

The following practices are basic building blocks for home–school–community collaboration:

- Promote a schoolwide instructional vision for cultural responsiveness and model these behaviors in classrooms, in hallways, and after school.
- Use data and community input to identify and replace policies, procedures, and practices that are exclusionary.
- Self-initiate two-way communication between instructional leaders, students, and community members in their preferred language and modality.
- Center student and community voices to assess and guide formation of goals, priorities, and strategies related to culturally responsive efforts.
- Leverage internal resources in conjunction with community partners to gain insight on the cultural backgrounds, perspectives, experiences, values, and needs of students and their local contexts.

Manage Input and Collective Decision Making

Culturally responsive approaches can be effective as a tactic to redistribute power and agency by designing meaningful opportunities for feedback and leadership. If we truly believe that communities are experts on their children and have their best interest in mind, then opportunities can and should be created to distribute power. Examples of powerful actions to support this strategy include the following:

- Invite student, family, or community representatives to participate on the school's instructional team or in other aspects of school governance.
- Invite community members to head up or cosponsor school-based initiatives, projects, or activities.
- Create opportunities for local organizations to facilitate professional development sessions with school-based educators.
- Proactively solicit community input and take feedback into account when enacting decisions.

Instructional leaders must be attuned to the needs of the students and their communities, actively looking to develop sustained and meaningful partnerships that affirm their contributions and the contents of their cultural backpacks. Building culturally affirming schools requires authentic and concerted efforts—not only for the sake of supporting and retaining educators of color, but also for nourishing and respecting students of color, their families, and their communities of origin.

Self-Assessment: Leadership for Culturally Responsive Approaches

This chapter provides several strategies across three categories to implement Principle 5: *Foster supportive environments for culturally responsive approaches*. See Figure 5.1 for a self-assessment you can use to evaluate strengths and opportunities for growth related to your current work as an instructional leader. It includes a rubric for the three categories (curriculum and instruction, teacher capacity and resources, and community partnerships) and each of the strategies addressed in this chapter.

Complete the rubric by identifying the value that aligns with your efforts to foster supportive environments for culturally responsive approaches. A score of 0 (No Evidence) indicates absence of the strategy. A score of 1 (Beginning) conveys intention and perhaps small-scale implementation, unsuccessful due to the barriers listed here or other factors. A score of 2 (Emerging) means implementation of strategy with occasional wins, sometimes undermined by barriers or other factors. A score of 3 (Progressing) indicates culturally responsive strategies are embedded into your daily work as an instructional leader and are accompanied by systems and routines to monitor their effectiveness and pivot as needed. A score of 4 (Innovating) indicates that these strategies are deeply integrated into the instructional culture of the school so that culturally responsive approaches are pronounced in all aspects of teaching and learning.

Conclusion

This chapter focuses on fostering supportive environments for culturally responsive approaches as a necessary commitment to support and retain a diverse educator workforce. Guided by the metaphor of the "cultural backpack," we have examined culturally responsive approaches as both a paradigm and collection of practices that center and honor the voices, experiences,

FIGURE 5.1

Self-Assessment: Culturally Responsive Approaches

	0	1	2	3	4
	No Evidence (absence of strategy)	**Beginning** (some small-scale implementation)	**Emerging** (occasional implementation)	**Progressing** (embedded in daily routines with some monitoring)	**Innovating** (deeply integrated in all aspects of instructional culture)
Curriculum and Instruction					
Enhance teacher autonomy	0	1	2	3	4
Center identity and criticality	0	1	2	3	4
Teacher Capacity and Resources					
Structure reflection and learning	0	1	2	3	4
Prioritize teacher planning and collaboration	0	1	2	3	4
Community Partnerships					
Facilitate home–school–community collaboration	0	1	2	3	4
Manage input and collective decision making	0	1	2	3	4

and cultural backgrounds of historically marginalized and minoritized communities. Influenced by contents of their own cultural backpacks, educators of color often demonstrate a unique sensitivity to implementing these approaches for the purposes of equitable representation in curriculum, positive identity development, piquing student interest and engagement, and helping students see school and learning as relevant to their everyday lives. Instructional leaders seeking to enact culturally affirming practices understand that all aspects of the school instructional culture must be responsive to the school's diverse students and staff, creating spaces where they feel welcome to express the fullness of their intersectional identities.

? Reflection Questions

1. Reflect on the contents of your cultural backpack. How do they inform your assumptions? Blind spots? Biases?
2. Consider the three barriers to fostering supporting environments for culturally responsive approaches—misunderstandings, standardization, and leadership assumptions. To what extent, if at all, do you encounter these barriers in your work?
3. Are there additional barriers that hamper the efforts of educators of color in your building to enact culturally responsive approaches? If so, what are they?
4. Consider the strategies offered in this chapter related to curriculum and instruction. What steps can you take to enhance teacher autonomy and center identity and criticality in curriculum and instruction?
5. Consider the strategies related to teacher capacity and resources offered in this chapter. In your own words, how might educators of color in your school and the students they serve benefit from these strategies? What partnership(s) or external resources might you secure to structure reflection and prioritize planning and collaboration? When can you start this work?
6. Community partnerships are a critical aspect to fostering a supportive environment for culturally responsive approaches. What can you do differently in the coming days or weeks to encourage more home–school–community collaboration and collective decision making?

🖐 Beyond the Text: Resources to Level Up

Cole-Malott, D.-M., Parker Thompson, K., Peterson-Ansari, R., Whitaker, R. W., II. (2021). *The Pennsylvania culturally relevant and sustaining education competencies.* Pennsylvania Educator Diversity Consortium. https://s3.amazonaws.com/newamericadotorg/documents/The_Pennsylvania_Culturally_Relevant_and_Sustaining_Education_Competencies.pdf

Coomer, M. N., Skelton, S. M., Kyser, T. S., Thorius, K. A. K., & Warren, C. (2017). *Assessing bias in standards and curricular materials.* Great Lakes Equity Center. https://greatlakesequity.org/resource/assessing-bias-standards-and-curricular-materials

Ferguson, L. (2015). *Evaluating American Indian materials and resources for the classroom.* Indian Education Division, Montana Office of Public Instruction. https://opi.mt.gov/Portals/182/Page%20Files/Indian%20Education/Indian%20Education%20101/Evaluating%20AI%20Materials%20and%20Resources%20for%20the%20Classroom.pdf

Muhammad, G. (2020). *Cultivating genius: An equity framework for culturally and historically responsive literacy.* Scholastic.

Peoples, L. Q., Islam, T., & Davis, T. (2021). *The culturally responsive-sustaining STEAM curriculum scorecard.* Metropolitan Center for Research on Equity and the Transformation of Schools, New York University. https://steinhardt.nyu.edu/sites/default/files/2021-02/CRSE-STEAMScorecard_FIN_optimized%20(1).pdf

6

PRINCIPLE 6:
Lead for an Inclusive Community

We have to stop thinking about diversity and start thinking about inclusion.

—Viola Davis

Diversity requires commitment. Achieving the superior performance diversity can produce needs further action—most notably, a commitment to develop a culture of inclusion.

—Alain Dehaze

Interviewer: How would you describe inclusion at your workplace?

Rosa: I feel like I have to put on an act at my job just to be accepted. I'm already cheery, but I feel like I have to amp it up and act super bubbly all the time. And you know what's strange? I feel like I shouldn't have to do that to belong, but that's the world we live in. It feels like there are no safe spaces for me to be myself until I get in my car at the end of the workday.

Alison: At work, it feels like I have to manage two things: my workload and the way I present myself. When I am talking with my white colleagues, I often find my voice and tone changing in ways that are different from what's natural for me. Sometimes, I don't even share my true opinion when asked because I don't want to receive backlash from my white colleagues—I just smile and agree. I don't do it on purpose, but I feel like I allow it to happen because if I don't, they are either going to get uncomfortable around me or they just won't understand me. But it makes me feel bad. It's like you're hiding a portion of yourself because you know that, depending on how you interact with the person, they will determine whether or not they understand you or whether or not they like you.

Throughout this book, we have drawn from teacher voices from the field as a source of insider knowledge about the ways many educators of color experience and navigate their schools. These interview excerpts from Rosa and Alison represent what is under the surface for many as they navigate isolation and challenging organizational conditions. Although the schools they work in may strive to employ a racially diverse educator workforce and wave the banner of acceptance, these narratives raise red flags about social belonging in the workplace and educators' ability to bring their true selves to their work. Unfortunately, Rosa and Alison are not outliers. Rather, their experiences are validated by a substantial research base, verbal and written testimonials from educators of color, and, anecdotally, countless conversations I have had as an instructional leader and teacher coach. Their stories are also consistent with my own experiences and observations as a former classroom teacher and instructional leader.

Nationally renowned educator, former White House principal ambassador fellow, and CEO of the Center for Black Educator Development Sharif El-Mekki (2022) makes a case that "recruiting Black teachers into a burning schoolhouse won't help to retain them." He uses the metaphor of a burning schoolhouse to describe organizational conditions that alienate, exclude, and push out educators of color. Quoting Pennsylvania teacher Kyle Epps, El-Mekki writes, "Hiring people of color is not enough to create culturally affirming schools. Schools need to have systems, programs and curriculum in place whose main goals are to foster and celebrate people of color" (paras. 13–14).

In line with this metaphor of the burning schoolhouse, we will examine a final call to action—one that entreats instructional leaders to attend to culturally affirming conditions in their schools.

The U.S. Department of Housing and Urban Development (n.d.) definition of inclusion states:

> **Inclusion** is a state of being valued, respected and supported. It's about focusing on the needs of every individual and ensuring the right conditions are in place for each person to achieve his or her full potential. Inclusion should be reflected in an organization's culture, practices and relationships that are in place to support a diverse workforce. Inclusion is the process of creating a working culture and environment that recognizes, appreciates, and effectively utilizes the talents, skills, and perspectives of every employee; uses employee skills to achieve the agency's objectives and mission; connects each employee to the organization; and encourages collaboration, flexibility, and fairness. We define inclusion as a set of behaviors (culture) that encourages employees to feel valued for their unique qualities and experience a sense of belonging. ***In simple terms, inclusion is getting the mix to work together.*** (paras. 5–6, emphasis in original)

Simply put, inclusion is a relational construct that examines how staff experience an organization, relate to each other, and function as a team.

This final chapter explores Principle 6: *Lead for an inclusive community*. We will also look at two concrete strategies to foster schoolwide commitment for culturally affirming schools: equity training and racial affinity spaces. Whereas Principles 4 and 5 focused largely on organizational dynamics regarding teaching and learning, Principle 6 encourages leaders to increase cultural competency and critical consciousness in staff. By themselves, strategies such as equity training and racial affinity spaces are not silver bullets; rather, they facilitate moving staff and other invested partners toward identifying and dismantling toxic structures in the workplace, enhancing cross-cultural understanding, and promoting social belonging for all, resulting in schools where educators can be their authentic selves and are seen, heard, and valued. Although different school types and settings may have different organizational expectations and constraints, the guidance in the following pages should help you advance your goal of leading a culturally affirming school to support and retain teachers of color.

Equity Training Explored

Kareem: I'm grateful for all the equity training that I had at my old school. I didn't see it then, but I see the differences between then and now with my new school. In my last school, it was like a family—everybody, including teachers, parents, students, and admin. At this school, we have it, but it doesn't seem to work. The way teachers speak about our Black and Latinx kids is atrocious—especially when the parents are not around! And because I stand up for our babies, I get thrown under the bus constantly. Makes me miss my last school so much. The staff was a bit more diverse than at my current school and we were professional with each other. We fostered positive relationships with each other. We really cared about each other. We learned from each other. We checked in on each other. There was just so much unity.

Equity training is a tool to advance intrapersonal and organizational cultural competence and critical consciousness among staff. Broadly, equity training includes mechanisms (e.g., coaching, professional development) that encourage the adoption of antibias and antiracist ideologies, behaviors, and praxis among staff. Equity trainings often explore the historical, social, organizational, and interpersonal dimensions of intersectional inequalities and stimulate reflection among participants to identify how these dimensions manifest in their communities of origin, everyday lives, and work. Sometimes referred to as antibias trainings, diversity workshops, or cultural competency professional development, equity training creates shared language and knowledge around concepts such as opportunity and resource gaps (see Chapter 1); colorblindness, bias, and racial microaggressions (see Chapter 2); and stereotypes and race-based assumptions (see Chapter 4). In these spaces, educators interrogate normalized assumptions and ahistorical truths—about themselves, their environment, or those from different ethnic-racial or cultural backgrounds—that they have breathed in like smog, whether they want to or not (Tatum, 2017). Equity training provides guidance on bridging cultural, class, and other social divides by learning from others of different backgrounds and identities. By sharing stories and gaining insight into how intersectional forces influence their daily lived experiences, educators can develop cultural competency and be inspired to act against inequality both inside and outside their classrooms. Equity training, when implemented correctly, can lead to healing, joy, and *in lak'ech,* a Maya-inspired concept explained by playwright and screenwriter Luis Valdez (1994) as "si te amo y respeto (if I love and respect you)/me amo y respeto yo (I love and respect myself)." Authentic equity training should foster a culturally affirming community that values and celebrates difference.

Defining Cultural Competence and Critical Consciousness

Cultural competence describes one's awareness and adeptness to engage across the lines of cultural differences (e.g., worldviews, beliefs, histories, values, traditions, practices). Cultural competence also encompasses an acute understanding of one's own cultural background and the ability to adapt attitudes and behaviors to navigate cultural mismatch, minimize miscommunication, and value the inherent dignity of others (DeAngelis, 2015). Culturally competent educators interrogate their preconceived notions to understand and appreciate cultural nuances expressed by colleagues, students, and members of the broader school community. Such interrogation of preconceived notions is a dynamic and continuous process, not one that is static or finite (Kumagai & Lypson, 2009).

Critical consciousness refers to the "ability to recognize and analyze systems of inequality and the commitment to take action against these systems" (El-Amin et al., 2017, para. 2; see also Freire, 1970). Critically conscious educators identify and uproot injustice and inequality for the purpose of advancing equity and the common good.

The Gap Between Intent and Impact

In my work, I encounter scores of educators who have sat through countless hours of equity training. Educators of color report that these trainings often overlook or minimize the effects of power and inequality on school dynamics and interpersonal working relationships. Kareem's, Rosa's, and Alison's narratives are consistent with these observations, revealing a gap between the intent of equity training and its actual effects on the day-to-day workplace experiences of educators of color. Professional learning consultant Nicole Tucker-Smith (2021) identifies three categories of training: (1) equity training that works, (2) equity training that *does not* work, and (3) equity training that appears to work but *actually does not.* Before we focus on indicators of successful equity training, we need to address the latter two categories.

As an instructional leader, it is fairly easy to identify a professional development or workshop that is not working: participants are disengaged, low-level chatter about everything other than the topic at hand fills the air, papers are being graded, and there may be an aura of confusion about the purpose of the workshop and how it connects to educators' everyday work. There may even be outright resistance to participation or verbal pushback against the workshop facilitator.

Equity training that appears successful but actually is not is much harder to detect. Tucker-Smith states:

> The third category is, in fact, the most dangerous, as it drains resources and creates a false sense of progress. Equity [training] that *appears* to work is deceiving and counterproductive. It can receive rave reviews from participants, but leaves individual biases and systemic barriers unchanged. (para. 2)

Tucker-Smith argues that successful facilitators of equity trainings go beyond raising awareness about inequality, pairing awareness with a commitment to change. Increasing cultural competency and critical consciousness requires self-reflection and impetus toward action. Participants who leave a training with "the mistaken impression that they are doing just fine" may have unchecked prejudices and stereotypes of which they are unaware (Kruger & Dunning, 1999, p. 1121). These individuals may perceive themselves to have a high level of cultural competence and critical consciousness as a result of their exposure to new information, but the acquisition of information has no bearing on how they relate to their students or colleagues.

Equity Training That Works

Equity training that works leads to personal, interpersonal, and organizational change because participants feel an individual and collective responsibility to dismantle inequality in their daily work. This type of equity training contains three important components:

1. Knowledge acquisition ("Today I learned . . .")
2. Relevance to praxis ("These are the implications as it relates to my work . . .")
3. Applicability ("As a result, I will take action by . . .")

Equity training should be more than an intellectual or emotional exercise; it should be an action-oriented activity guided by new knowledge. Katerina Bezrukova and colleagues (2016) carried out a meta-analysis of 40 years of research on equity training, concluding that equity trainings that incorporate knowledge and action over a sustained period bear the greatest potential for personal and organizational transformation. On the other hand, Bezrukova states, "if you don't do it right, you can get a lot of horrible and tragic outcomes" (as quoted in Guy, 2019, p. 52).

Leading for Inclusion Through Equity Training

Equity training offerings are diverse and multimodal. Examples include asynchronous webinars, in-person training, book clubs, synchronous web-based courses, and other approaches. Many equity trainings are free and available on the internet for public consumption. Some districts and schools employ a one-size-fits-all approach to equity training, while others generate customized in-house trainings designed to target individual needs. In the absence of leadership capacity, equity trainings can be designed and facilitated by external providers and consultants.

Despite the plethora of delivery options, however, many equity training programs pay little attention to learning science or organizational theory (Cheng et al., 2019). The next section identifies 10 indicators of equity training that works, along with recommendations to coordinate and manage such training. The list is not intended to address the best equity training programs, curricula, or sequencing—though all of these topics are critically important—but to provide transferable guidelines and examples of best practices that can be applied across school types and settings.

As you read the list, consider each indicator in the context of your school. Ask yourself: Are these best practices in place in my school context?

How does implementation support staff knowledge acquisition, relevance to praxis, and applicability? Following the list of indicators, you will be invited to draw on your understanding by analyzing a case study.

Ten Indicators of Equity Training That Works

Indicator 1: Goal-Oriented

Equity trainings must include specific and concrete goals. Concrete data undergird the rationale behind a focus on equity and drive goal design. Ideally, goals should support other schoolwide priorities and encourage measurable change in adult behaviors. Goals should be communicated explicitly and often. In the context of equity training, facilitators connect training topics and outcomes to larger goals. The Illinois State Board of Education (ISBE, n.d.) provides an example of goal-oriented equity training by instructing leaders to create concrete goals that align with local and state initiatives as well as design progress monitoring to assess progress made toward these goals.

Indicator 2: Explicit Strategy

Leaders of effective equity training consistently communicate why equity training matters, the significance of training topics, and implications for the building or network. Through written, face-to-face, or formal communication, they give a clear rationale about the purpose of training, expectations for educators, and how this strategy supports broader district and school goals. Leaders anchor their work within the larger context of advancing equitable outcomes for and with members of the school community. Furthermore, the equity training provides a road map for members of the school community to collaboratively adopt equity as a mindset and aspect of their practice. Simply put, clear and frequent messaging ensures the significance of equity training does not become muddled in the daily hubbub of school.

Indicator 3: Diverse Representation

Facilitators of effective equity training reflect different backgrounds in terms of ethnicity, race, and other aspects of identity. Some claim the utility of multiple facilitators (two at a minimum) who have experience leading research-based equity work, are able to anticipate and attend to a spectrum of participant reactions, and represent dominant and nondominant identities of school community members. For one such example, see the Illinois State Board of Education Diversity Equity and Inclusion Provider Evaluation Tool linked to at the end of this chapter. For a school with predominantly Latino/x students and majority white staff, the facilitators might represent a cross-cultural duo with lived experiences and insider knowledge about staff and student groups. This kind of ethnic-racial parity between trainers and participants is associated with positive outcomes, including greater credibility (Gardenswartz & Rowe, 1997).

Indicator 4: Linked to Measurable Outcomes

Effective equity training is designed and facilitated with the needs of the school in mind. Determining those needs can be accomplished using the School Readiness Tool from Figure 3.2 or another needs assessment. Instructional leaders then partner with session facilitators to design trainings with specific outcomes tailored to produce personal, interpersonal, or organizational change. Mechanisms such as pre and post surveys are used to stimulate participants' reflection on their learning and gauge the influence of training on their practice. Data can lead to pivots regarding topic selection or facilitation approach.

Coauthors and equity training facilitators Tracey Benson and Sarah Fiarman (n.d.) recommend three approaches to monitoring data and outcomes:

1. *Assess participant knowledge and practice related to each session outcome.* Creating survey questions geared toward participant satisfaction may provide misleading data regarding the efficacy of equity training. Some trainings may invoke necessary discomfort in the process of inducing long-term change. In addition, a generic survey may not be conducive to assessing session outcomes. Instead, pursue participant feedback on the session outcome and its impact on professional practice, focusing on knowledge and skills participants took from the time instead of their emotional reactions to the session.

2. *Collect and store data over time to determine trends.* Use a spreadsheet to visualize data collected, such as session outcomes, survey items or questions, and accompanying responses.

3. *Disaggregate by participant demographics (e.g., content area, non-tenure vs. tenure, race/ethnicity, gender) when analyzing data.* Apply this strategy to notice trends within and across equity trainings over time. Analyze trends and disparities in data as they relate to the experiences of different groups. This practice requires pre-identifying demographics and data points of interest that you want to learn more about.

Indicator 5: Opportunities for Participant Engagement

Effective equity training offers frequent occasions for participant engagement around the meatiest portions of the session to deepen knowledge and skill. Examples of participant engagement include structured opportunities to respond to or pose questions, peer discussion, and self-assessment of learning. Engagement prompts deeper personal reflection, responsibility, and accountability regarding issues undergirding intersectionality and inequality. Instead of passively presenting new information, Tucker-Smith (2021) recommends educators engage in inquiry, interrogate their personal beliefs and practice, and pursue solutions to apply equity training skills to their context.

Indicator 6: Relational Trust

Leaders intentionally cultivate opportunities to foster interpersonal trust with participants and among participants. Trust is a prerequisite to vulnerability and openness to learn, particularly in cross-cultural spaces or in situations susceptible to fractured working relationships. In effective equity training, leaders design or coconstruct a program with facilitators and/or participants, reinforcing interpersonal agreements for session participants. Glenn Singleton and Cyndie Hays (2008) secure four agreements to foster trust and vulnerability in participants in what they call "courageous conversation" about race: (1) stay engaged, (2) expect to experience discomfort, (3) speak your truth, and (4) expect and accept a lack of closure. Equity training design can foster trust by building on agreements like these. In their equity training sessions, Millicent Jeanette Carvalho-Grevious and Tawana Ford Sabbath (2018) lead engagement opportunities that evoke parallel emotions and connections to the human condition for participants, regardless of their background. After participants recognize and acknowledge their shared experiences, Carvalho-Grevious and Ford Sabbath segue into challenging topics such as race and microaggressions.

Indicator 7: Actionable Next Steps

Effective equity trainings culminate with clear, actionable next steps related to training outcomes. These next steps are manageable and suited for educators at all entry points. Leaders institute systematic follow-through and accountability to minimize the gap between knowledge and practice. Examples of next steps include self-directed learning, mentorship, or practical suggestions that are curated to align with participants' professional roles and contexts (ISBE, n.d.).

Indicator 8: Effective Facilitation

Indicators of effective facilitation include equitable participation during training, transfer of key learnings to participants, and participant support during and after training. When necessary, leaders provide coaching or feedback to enhance the quality of equity training. Leaders should expect facilitators to manage participants' emotional responses and resistance. Among white participants, resistance may manifest as "blame and shame," resentment, guilt, or allegations of reverse racism, which, if unchecked, can undermine participant learning. In addition to facilitating discussion, trainers can model introspection and vulnerability through personal anecdotes and examples that align with the equity training content.

Indicator 9: Continuity and Cohesion

Effective equity training is based on well-regarded, research-based materials and resources. Equity training is not a one-stop shop. Rather, trainings follow a logical progression, outcomes build on each other in complexity from one training to the next, and prior learning and skills are constantly reinforced. Each training session is accompanied by clearly communicated next steps, accountability, and support. Moreover, equity training topics are reinforced in other school contexts (e.g., department meetings, initiatives). There is clear accountability and follow-up after each session. These qualities are consistent with findings by Marc Bendick and colleagues (2001), who conclude that integrated and sustained trainings are more effective than ones disconnected from other initiatives.

Indicator 10: Leadership Commitment and Accountability

Leaders demonstrate commitment to equity training by being present, engaging as a participant, and modeling behaviors such as inquiry, vulnerability, and personal reflection. Leadership attitude and behaviors signal that equity training is important, even when leaders face competing priorities or unanticipated interruptions. Leaders also model personal accountability and adjust policy, personal practice, or procedure to enhance equity. One misconception is that leaders should refrain from participating in the training so that teachers can talk freely, without a sense of oversight. However, Shannon Cheng and colleagues (2019) argue, "The success of diversity training depends on visible and active leadership, organizational culture, and motivation. Leadership participation and valuing diversity training improves the effectiveness of diversity trainings" (p. 8).

Although this list is not intended to be exhaustive, the quality indicators provide a basic framework to guide implementation and evaluation of equity training.

What About Attendance?

A common question is "Should equity training be voluntary or mandatory?" Mandatory attendance is linked with higher effectiveness (Bendick et al., 2001; Rynes & Rosen, 1995). However, making participation voluntary may help mitigate backlash among resistant staff. These conflicting outcomes call for serious consideration of how expectations surrounding participation can strengthen or undermine diversity training as a means of improving organizational conditions.

Equity Training Case Study: Disgruntled Participants

Now we will put together what we have gleaned and apply our learning to a case study. After reading the case study, work independently or with a team to answer the questions.

Case Study

Imagine you are the professional development leader of a midsize suburban middle school. Although the district has historically consisted of mainly white middle-class and working-class families, it has experienced significant demographic shifts in the last 10 years. Large numbers of English language learners and Black and Latino/x students are now moving into the district. Staff racial demographics remain mostly white, although two new Black teachers, a Navajo teacher, and an Asian teacher have recently joined the 30-person staff. Each of these teachers has previous experience working with racially diverse students in urban and suburban settings.

Due to state department of education initiatives adopted in 2020, your district has worked with an outside provider for two years to develop and facilitate quarterly equity trainings for the whole staff. Equity training topics are selected based on a needs assessment performed in the prior school year, and trainings include annual goals as well as measurable outcomes for each session.

In years past, facilitators have not collected survey data to assess the equity training and gauge participants' experiences. However, you recently read *Support and Retain Educators of Color: 6 Principles for Culturally Affirming Leadership* and learned the importance of assessing training outcomes, so you collaborated with training facilitators to distribute a participant survey. In a recent meeting, facilitators shared the initial survey data. You noticed that, by and large, participants had mixed feelings about the training. They also made some comments that you found particularly alarming. These responses appear in Figure 6.1.

As the professional development leader, read the participant responses and answer the following questions:

1. What are the underlying issues at hand?
2. What steps can you take to address this situation?

FIGURE 6.1
Responses Pulled from Equity Training Assessment Survey

> *I really like our equity trainings. I find the presenters kind and personable. My only problem is that it often feels like once we have the training, it just goes on that hill and dies there. We only talk about race in professional development, and I don't really see anything coming out of it.*

> *Equity training is touch and go for me mostly because I feel like the buy-in among staff isn't always there. I've noticed that some voices dominate the conversations, so it's hard to see to what extent the rest of the staff are getting anything out of it. Although I personally have learned a lot, I feel like people are reluctant to share anything about themselves—it's all abstract and surface-level.*

> *At the end of our trainings, I feel really emotionally exhausted. I don't see how what is discussed within the context of professional development is monitored or supposed to translate to our practice.*

> *To be honest, I don't see the purpose of these trainings, which is why I'm so disengaged. I'm not walking away from these sessions with information that I didn't already know. Then, at the end, we just have a reflection question and then—BOOM—we're done at three o'clock. I get so frustrated because the assumption is that the conversation about race can be shut off, when these issues are always present in my life.*

3. How might you coordinate with others (e.g., external provider, leadership team, staff) to improve the equity training?
4. What steps can you take to improve your leadership of equity training in the future?
5. What issues stand out to you as either positive or negative factors in this training?
6. To what extent, if at all, do you see evidence of the 10 indicators of effective equity training in this case study?

Drawing from the case study description and participant responses, it appears necessary to improve facilitation (Indicator 8) by encouraging equitable participation. There is also an absence of relational trust (Indicator 6), which leads one to wonder about training norms and the extent to which they are consistently reinforced. There is also a broader concern about the presence of actionable next steps (Indicator 7), which raises the question of what follow-up looks like and how training participants are supported in seeing the relevance between equity training topics and their everyday practice.

Based on your experiences and observations, what other quality indicators are absent in this case study? What do you wonder about the equity training in this scenario?

Final Thoughts: Equity Training

Equity training is a strategy to support Principle 6: *Lead for an inclusive community.* In response to rapid student diversification in preK–12 schools across the nation, many state and local entities mandate equity training as a component of professional development. Although such training is often contextualized as a mechanism to improve student outcomes, effective equity training should also drive personal, interpersonal, and organizational change; educators of all backgrounds should commit to enhancing equity in their everyday work and strive to improve in-school experiences for students and for each other. By promoting the relevance of equity training to everyday interactions and relationships inside and outside the classroom, instructional leaders demonstrate culturally affirming leadership practices and inspire educators to mobilize for equity.

Racial Affinity Spaces

Grace: I wish that there was a space for us to meet each other. It would be great for some of the younger teachers to get guidance from the older, more veteran teachers. I think creating that type of community would have been so beneficial for me in the early years—and even now! I also think it would have helped me to feel more confident by understanding experiences that I had when I first started teaching.

A second strategy to support leading for an inclusive community is the creation of racial affinity groups in your school. Affinity groups are gatherings of individuals of similar backgrounds and interests to make meaning of shared experiences and collaborate around common goals. Citing examples such as content-area teams and grade-level groups, Micia Mosely (Warren-Grice, 2021) argues that schools already contain many types of affinity groups in which educators learn from each other and work together to support their students. Likewise, racial affinity groups function as a safe space to engage with others who have experienced similar racialized and organizational experiences. A growing body of literature underscores the benefits of participation in racial affinity groups and supports them as a strategy to retain a diverse teacher workforce (Bristol et al., 2020; Kohli, 2019; Mosely, 2018; Pour-Khorshid, 2018).

Education-based racial affinity groups have an extensive history. In her 2021 report *A Space to Be Whole,* April Warren-Grice historicizes racial affinity groups in the 19th and 20th centuries as spaces where educators of color gathered for empowerment, resource sharing, and advocacy work to expand access and opportunity for the communities they served. Another example can be found in the Black educator groups that organized to support the NAACP in acquiring the evidence needed for the landmark 1954 Supreme Court case *Brown v. Board of Education of Topeka,* illustrating the potential of affinity groups to be antiracist spaces responsive to the needs of "specific racialized group[s that] experience the consequences of institutionalized racism in particular ways" (Mosely, 2018, para. 16).

Benefits of Racial Affinity Groups

By design, racial affinity groups help schools advance their goals of cultural affirmation and inclusion. Racial affinity groups provide educators of color with an opportunity to learn from, exchange ideas with, and build community with other educators who have similar backgrounds, daily experiences, and aspirations. In these spaces, educators of color can

> gather and be free from the mainstream stereotypes and marginalization that permeate every other societal space we occupy. [Racial affinity

groups are] spaces where we can be our authentic selves without white people's judgment and insecurity muzzling that expression. We need spaces where we can simply be—where we can get off the treadmill of making white people comfortable and finally realize just how tired we are. (Blackwell, 2018, para. 3)

In these safe spaces, educators of color can focus on themselves—their achievements, their aspirations, their needs—without the need to defend, rationalize, or accommodate their white colleagues in multiracial spaces. Racial affinity groups allow educators of color to draw inspiration and empowerment to sustain them in the work, combating the racial isolation that occurs when an educator of color is the "one and only" or "one of a few" educators of color in their building or district.

A common misconception is that racial affinity spaces are merely places to air grievances. That is not the case. Rather, racial affinity spaces entail a clear purpose and structured activities to build educators' capacity, buffer against racialized experiences, and navigate school organizational dynamics. Carvalho-Grevious and Ford Sabbath (2018) discuss an affinity session with Black coworkers they facilitated titled "Microaggressions and Microinequities in Social Work Practice." After talking about barriers and challenges in the workplace, participants also walked away with self-care strategies and a plan to secure a mentor—concrete strategies to navigate instances of race and class-based harm in the workplace.

Some racial affinity groups are referred to as *caucuses* because of their emphasis on political engagement and activism (Blitz & Kohl, 2012). More than 200 registered racial affinity groups for educators of color nationwide as of 2021 (including Hawaii and Puerto Rico) engage in this type of organizing and advocacy work (Warren-Grice, 2021). For example, the Institute for Teachers of Color Committed to Racial Justice (ITOC) is a nationwide organization in which educators of color participate in yearlong critical professional development designed to "support well-being, strengthen racial literacy, and cultivate the racial justice leadership capacities of teachers of color who work in K–12 public schools that serve students of color" (ITOC, n.d.). ITOC participants also build community with a cohort of like-minded educators of color and receive professional mentorship from another educator of color.

In this manner, racial affinity groups can lead to the formation of meaningful interpersonal relationships within the context of a larger group.

Another example of racial affinity groups engaging in organizing and advocacy work is the Teachers of Color Foundation in Edmonds, Washington, which holds monthly events for educators of color within the Edmonds School District as well as mentoring, career development, and even access to professional development funds to meet pedagogical needs and interests unmet by the district. Delegates from the Teachers of Color Foundation meet with leaders to provide input on policies related to the recruitment, support, and retention of educators of color. In one instance, the foundation worked for two years with the district's human resources department to amend interviewing protocols, resulting in a diversification of the teacher workforce—subsequently, one in five new hires identified as a person of color (Warren-Grice, 2021). Together, these examples convey how racial affinity groups foster agency among teachers of color and advance education equity.

Racial affinity groups are also an effective strategy for white educators. Just as educators of color need a confidential and safe space to share their racialized organizational experiences, affinity groups allow white educators to discuss issues of power, reflect on racial privilege, and examine how the social construct of race influences their work, as well as explore the emotional responses that accompany this introspective work. In these contexts, white educators can actively advance their own understanding of ethnic-racial topics in community with like-minded white colleagues without demanding psychological or emotional labor from educators of color. Affinity groups also equip white educators with the tools to engage in courageous conversations about race, moving beyond acknowledging truths of intersectional inequality to act as coconspirators alongside their colleagues of color.

Figure 6.2 summarizes the benefits of racial affinity groups for both educators of color and white educators.

Different Forms of Racial Affinity Groups

I often come across school and district leaders who are intrigued by the idea of racial affinity groups, but unsure about how to get started. I have also met leaders who are perplexed about how to implement affinity groups, particularly in contexts in which there is only one educator of color in a school

FIGURE 6.2
Racial Affinity Group Benefits

Educators of Color	White Educators
• Provides confidential, affirming, collaborative space to share experiences and challenges • Centers the needs, values, and humanity of educators of color • Enables targeted skill acquisition and career development • Fosters collaboration and resource sharing with respect to educator goals and identity • Facilitates networking, community building, and organizing	• Provides confidential space to reflect, ask questions, and learn about inequality • Builds knowledge regarding historical and contemporary inequalities in and outside of education • Enables the acquisition of practical tools to dismantle inequality • Promotes coconspiratorship and mutually reinforcing activities with racial affinity groups for educators of color

or a few educators of color scattered across a district, making in-person meetings impractical. Racial affinity groups can take many forms; consider the ones described below if you are faced with these or other challenges. Some groups target specific racial groups (e.g., Black educators, Asian American educators), while others focus on overlapping identities (e.g., Latina/x women, Black men) or multiple ethnic/racial groups (e.g., African, Latino/x, Asian, and Native American [ALANA] groups).

Affinity Professional Development

Groups that participate in racial affinity professional development (PD) fall into three overlapping categories: social justice–oriented PD, critical PD, and pedagogical and instructional PD. Social justice–oriented PD focuses on topics such as racial justice and other forms of intersectional inequality. Critical PD spans a variety of topics (e.g., self-care, racial identity development) and "frames teachers as politically-aware individuals who have a stake [in] transforming society" (Kohli et al., 2021, p. 89). Pedagogical and instructional PD is designed to equip teachers with training, coaching, material resources, and access to experts in instructional approaches (e.g., culturally sustaining pedagogy, abolitionist teaching) that are unavailable at their school sites. One example is the Pennsylvania-based Mirrors in Education, which hosts stand-alone professional development targeted toward educators of color on topics such as inclusive education, conflict resolution, and incorporating social media into the classroom.

Web-Based Communities

Many educators connect through web-based platforms using technology such as videoconferencing to establish nationwide racial affinity spaces. Organizations such as Black Male Educators (BMEs) Talk and The Black Teacher Project host social media forums to share resources, exchange ideas, and build community. BMEs Talk also hosts Twitter chats to encourage conversation and collaboration around chosen topics. Using these platforms, educators of color can develop meaningful bonds with other educators of color despite geographic distance.

Regional Racial Affinity Groups

Many racial affinity groups are comprised of educators that work at the same school. However, racial affinity groups can also span multiple sites (e.g., meeting locations rotate) or draw from an entire district. Multisite and district racial affinity groups ameliorate concerns that arise when there are few educators of color in one school. One such example is Kirkwood Teachers of Color Group, a St. Louis–based collective open to educators of color in the Kirkwood School District. Racial affinity groups can also be designated by area. For example, the Southeastern PA Educators of Color Network brings together educators of color and leaders from local school districts and institutions of higher education to network, collaborate, and share their experiences during quarterly affinity dinners.

Identity-Based Mentoring, Leadership, and Advancement Programs

Data collected by the National Center for Education Statistics (2022) reveal that educators of color remain underrepresented in positions of school leadership. To address this void, racial affinity groups such as the Boston Public Schools Women Educators of Color (WEOC) Executive Coaching Leadership Program are designed to recruit and retain educators of color in leadership. The WEOC (and its counterpart affinity group for men of color) supports lateral and vertical movement into leadership and is open to self-identified women of color with at least three years' service in the district. While enrolled in the program, participants complete graduate coursework, experience executive coaching, and engage in activities to enhance leadership skills, such as public speaking and critical thinking. Upon completion of the program, participants receive a graduate certificate from a local college.

Problems of Practice Groups

Many racial affinity groups focus on a shared problem of practice to drive their programming and organizing work. Mosely (2018) recalls a year-long book study facilitated by The Black Teacher Project to analyze Zaretta Hammond's (2015) *Culturally Responsive Teaching and the Brain.* In workshops guided by a veteran Black educator, the racial affinity group explored neuroscience and racial identity and how they intersected with the group's perceptions of their own cultural background and the backgrounds of their students. Participants described their engagement in this racial affinity group as fulfilling personal interests and professional needs unmet by their schools. Racial affinity groups can also use articles, podcasts, or films linked to a shared problem of practice to guide their discussion (Michael & Conger, 2009). Problems of practice might even focus on specific timely issues such as police brutality or immigration.

Other Formats

In addition to the diverse types of racial affinity groups mentioned in this section, racial affinity groups can have a variety of leadership structures. To build capacity, instructional leaders can designate an outside facilitator, delegate internal leadership, or support rotating facilitators. Instructional leaders can also sponsor educators of color to participate in regional or web-based affinity spaces or allocate professional development funds and release time to attend affinity-based professional development or conferences.

As mentioned earlier, there are over 200 racial affinity groups located in the United States. Many of these entities can be found through a racial affinity group directory located at LiberatedGenius.com. The time is now for instructional leaders to enhance their support of racial affinity groups and dismantle barriers so that educators of color have access to resources, communities, and spaces that affirm their humanity. As Kelsey Blackwell (2018) writes, "valuing and protecting spaces for people of color (PoC) is not just a kind thing that white people can do to help us feel better; supporting these spaces is crucial to the resistance of oppression" (para. 4).

Addressing Critiques of Racial Affinity Groups

Despite a growing supportive research base and testimonials from educators of color about the rejuvenating qualities of racial affinity groups, skepticism and targeted attacks continue to second-guess the validity of this strategy. Inside schools, naysayers may question the efficacy of implementing racial affinity groups to achieve ethnic-racial and cultural unity. Let's look at some ubiquitous critiques and their counterarguments.

Critique: Racial Affinity Groups for People of Color Are Just a Blaming Session

At their core, racial affinity groups for people of color are intended to provide support, wellness, and empowerment in community with those of similar ethnic-racial backgrounds in spaces designed for them. They offer healing through introspection, resource sharing, and collaboration. Framing racial affinity spaces as "blaming sessions" overlooks the value obtained by making meaning from shared experiences and developing actionable techniques to sustain educators of color in their work.

Critique: Racial Affinity Groups Make White People Feel Shameful About Racism

As white people explore their racial identity and deepen their understanding about the effects racial constructs have on their work, they will likely experience a host of emotional responses. Racial affinity groups for white educators can create a safe space for exploring these emotions. The goal, however, is to gain practical guidance for moving beyond acknowledging inequality to what Bettina Love (2019) describes as "courageous co-conspiratorship" in which white educators "understand their privilege and work to challenge and undo patriarchy" and other forms of intersectional inequalities (p. 118).

Critique: How Are We Supposed to Be Inclusive If We Separate (Segregate)?

Critics never fail to bring up the false equivalency of racial affinity groups with segregation. The institution of segregation was developed by white American policymakers to maintain a racial and social hierarchy and kept intact by the 1896 *Plessy v. Ferguson* Supreme Court ruling in favor of state-sanctioned segregation. When state-sanctioned segregation was overturned, communities of color were integrated into dominantly Eurocentric spaces, often not on their own terms (Lutz, 2017). Therefore, racial affinity groups are designed to equip educators of color to re-enter and thrive in spaces not designed for them! Likewise, white educators can explore their racial identity, confront their racial privilege, and deconstruct the power imbalances to foster authentic relationships with students and colleagues whose backgrounds differ from their own (Love, 2019).

Leading for Inclusion Through Racial Affinity Spaces

As an instructional leader, the possibilities of affinity groups are numerous. Leaders can allocate professional development funds to pay member fees for educators of color to join organizations such as Latinos for Education or sponsor teachers to attend conferences like the Black Men Educators Convening, held annually in Philadelphia. Instructional leaders can also collaborate with other schools or institutions of higher education to generate regional affinity spaces and foster cross-campus conversation and collaboration, as is the case with the Southeastern PA Educators of Color Network (SPECN), which partners with Villanova University. Coordinating with established nonprofits and organizations with extensive expertise in establishing racial affinity groups has never been easier, thanks to the online directory at LiberatedGenius.com assembled by April Warren-Grimes.

You may be curious about forming racial affinity groups for educators of color at your school. You may also find the idea of white educators accessing racial affinity groups to support their journey toward cultural competence and critical consciousness compelling. The following five questions will help you get started with the planning process.

1. What key issues need to be addressed?

The first step in the planning process is to identify the issue or issues you are trying to tackle through racial affinity groups. The issues you identify will shape the design of the racial affinity group. Revisit the concerns brought up by educators of color in your school assessment, surveys, or pulse meetings (see Chapter 3). For example, did educators express desire for additional instructional support, such as coaching or professional development? If so, you might implement affinity-based PD. Consider disaggregating educator concerns; for example, have early-career educators of color expressed different needs than mid-career educators? Early-career educators may benefit from exchanging successful classroom practices and resources with other early-career teachers. Mid-career educators may want a space to discuss broader equity issues in the school and build coalitions. In this manner, establish different types of affinity spaces for the respective groups. If you do not have a clear idea of the key issues that need to be addressed, consider forming a task force. Identifying key issues will help determine the goals and agenda of racial affinity groups in your school.

2. What is the best way to communicate the purpose of racial affinity groups?

Clear, proactive communication is necessary to convey the importance of racial affinity groups, explain benefits for school staff, and encourage buy-in prior to launch. One compelling description of racial affinity groups comes from the National Equity Project (n.d.), which defines racial affinity groups as spaces that

> support people to do their own reflection, learning, growth and healing with others positioned similarly in a system of racism (or other facet of oppression)—building relationships and processing what is most needed and meaningful for them given their identities. When affinity spaces are created alongside ongoing "alone" work and thoughtful supports to

come together across differences of identity, conditions can be strengthened for a more honest and liberated multiracial/multicultural community. (para. 1)

You may also consider explaining some of the key issues or data that led to the implementation of racial affinity groups in your school context. Refer staff to resources and readings such as Blackwell's (2018) "Why People of Color Need Spaces Without White People," which excellently conveys the necessity of racial solidarity for healing and rejuvenation, asking, "Why wouldn't an ally be in support of this?"

It may also be helpful to communicate clear boundaries, explaining what racial affinity spaces are intended to accomplish versus what they are *not* intended to accomplish. For example, racial affinity spaces do not replace human resources norms regarding workplace discrimination or harassment. When you propose implementing racial affinity groups, be prepared to address questions and concerns, for example, about who can participate, how confidentiality will be assured, and why the groups are necessary. Also be prepared to address concerns about affinity groups being exclusionary or promoting racial segregation.

3. What logistics and resources are needed now to get racial affinity groups off the ground? What logistics and resources will be needed in the future to ensure racial affinity groups are accessible, are sustainable, and accomplish their intended purpose?

Time, a critical factor for all educators, is also a necessary consideration for a functioning racial affinity group. At least 60 minutes should be allocated for an effective affinity group meeting. This time should not conflict with other teacher responsibilities or planning time. You may want to survey prospective participants to ensure the time selected is conducive to their schedule. For example, a teacher lunch period of 75 minutes may provide sufficient time for groups to meet, allowing for transition time as well. However, lunch duty for even part of the lunch block undermines a teacher's ability to access the racial affinity group. After-school activities, meeting with students, and life responsibilities may also prevent educators from meeting outside their contracted hours. Establishing racial affinity groups may require incorporating the practice as a nonnegotiable component of the school master schedule to ensure that educators are able to participate. As an instructional leader, you will have to consider how to eliminate potential barriers so that all educators can participate.

Location is another logistical consideration. The spaces in which affinity groups meet should be comfortable and quiet: spaces where confidential conversations can be held and meetings will be uninterrupted.

Financial and human resources are also critical. Facilitators should be amply compensated for their labor. If groups meet outside the confines of the school day, professional development funds may be used to compensate educators for their time. Monies may also be allocated to expenses such as food and beverages. Finally, because racial affinity groups are linked to personal and professional development, additional funds may be allocated for materials (e.g., books for book study) or other resources needed to accomplish their agenda.

4. Who is best equipped to lead and facilitate this work?

Cultural competency and organizational proficiency are two essential qualities for guiding this work. Facilitators should reflect the backgrounds of the participants and be people who can build rapport and share cultural knowledge with the group. Facilitators should have experience in navigating interpersonal and group dynamics. You may consider assessing interest in the task among your staff or bring in an external organization to facilitate the groups. You may even want to ask staff to nominate colleagues or an outside facilitator to take on the role.

5. What is my role in supporting coalition work?

It bears repeating that the goal of racial affinity groups is to mobilize around shared goals and purposes. Instructional leaders play a critical role in ensuring that racial affinity groups are widely accessible to all interested educators. Your task is to be a lead advocate for the racial affinity groups, providing educators of color the undivided time, material resources, and financial support needed to pursue their activities. This responsibility also requires planning ahead to commit to resources racial affinity groups may need when they pivot to address new issues or needs that arise. If your school launches multiple racial affinity groups, support intergroup alliances and coalition building, which might include building time into the calendar for groups to come together, share their learnings, and strategize around mutually reinforcing activities.

Leaders must also be personally responsive and accountable to their racial affinity groups, make time to engage in listening sessions, receive direct feedback, and generate input on schoolwide policies and practices that affect educators, students, and their families. Failure to apply input from racial affinity groups undermines the practice of using the groups to improve organizational conditions and experiences for all staff.

Final Thoughts: Racial Affinity Groups

In Chapter 2, I shared the story of Leslie, a biracial educator with 10 years of experience across suburban and urban schools. Early in her career, she described being surrounded by "school mothers," veteran Black women teachers who took her under their wing, showed her the ropes regarding connecting with students and their families, and encouraged her to pursue her love of teaching reading to become a reading specialist. This informal network illustrates the power of racial affinity groups as spaces to encourage personal and professional development.

When Leslie accepted a new position as a reading specialist and changed schools, she felt the absence of her school mothers and faced a hostile environment tempered with gendered and racist microaggressions. Without the affinity support, she says, "there was no way I could do it anymore," and she left the profession temporarily, choosing to return several years later. Leslie described teaching as her life's vocation; she felt she was called to teach in the community where she grew up so that children could experience having a teacher that not only looked like them but grew up in similar circumstances. One can only wonder how racial affinity groups might have filled the void of support Leslie felt in her second school. Perhaps racial affinity groups might have provided her a safe space to share her concerns and discuss how she had been treated, or equipped her with strategies and resources to navigate the challenges she faced. At the end of the day, Leslie experienced an absence of support and isolation that no educator deserves. As instructional leaders, we have a moral imperative to do better.

Conclusion

So what happens now?

What are you *doing* to ensure that educators of color are thriving in your school?

How will you *apply* the strategies in this book to support and retain educators of color?

This book focuses on a critical issue affecting schools and students in public schools across the United States. Nationwide, educators of color remain vastly underrepresented and outnumbered by their white colleagues, who comprise nearly 80 percent of the teacher workforce. Over half of the students enrolled in K–12 schools in the United States are students of color— and this number is growing quickly. Moreover, disproportionate turnover among educators of color in comparison with white teachers continues to undermine initiatives to diversify the field of teaching—a disservice to all students, regardless of their background. When asked about their premature departure from their schools and from teaching, educators of color cite leadership behaviors, insufficient instructional support, lack of autonomy, and other factors linked to racialized organizational experiences that pushed them out of teaching. These areas *can* and *need to be* transformed to support and retain educators of color.

This text offers six principles for instructional leaders to guide their work to make their schools culturally affirming.

Principle 1: *Acknowledge that educator diversity matters* provided a historical, social, and political context for increasing the diversity of the teacher workforce. We came to understand that diversifying the teacher workforce is not only necessary to match the rich and growing ethnic-racial and cultural diversity of our students but also critical in enriching teaching and learning, school–community relationships, and the overall functioning of the school community.

Principle 2: *Cultivate reflection and self-awareness* led us to consider how the social constructs of race and racism are deeply entrenched factors that shaped schools historically and continue to influence the landscape of teaching today. We also learned three strategies—interrogate biases, understand intent and impact, and consider intersectionality—as foundational elements to prompt personal reflection and self-awareness about how race influences our work as instructional leaders.

Principle 3: *Assess and plan for action* brought forward systematic data collection and analysis tools to identify personal, interpersonal, and organizational barriers that undermine efforts to diversify the teacher workforce. Guided by quantitative data, anecdotal information, and information gathering from teachers of color, we looked at ways to develop an action plan to address the barriers to fostering an inclusive school.

Principle 4: *Commit to sustainable and high-impact instructional supports* explored how issues such as race-based assumptions, stereotypes, and low expectations combined with limits on leadership capacity often leave educators of color without consistent instructional support. In turn, pedagogical expertise, professional capacity, and personal well-being were offered as three areas in which leaders of support can directly facilitate, organize, or coordinate support that targets the needs of teachers of color and communicates that their professional growth matters.

Principle 5: *Foster supportive environments for culturally responsive approaches* explored the types of teacher beliefs and practices that seek to facilitate consciousness raising, dismantle Eurocentrism, and integrate students' cultural backgrounds with teaching and learning. Despite the benefits associated with culturally responsive approaches to education, multiple studies indicate that teachers of color often encounter barriers and lack of support in implementing these pedagogies at their school and with their students. Strategies in three key areas—curriculum and instruction, teacher capacity and resources, and community partnerships—were offered to navigate these barriers.

Principle 6: *Lead for an inclusive community* called our attention to equity training and racial affinity groups as strategies to mobilize staff as critical partners in advancing culturally responsive conditions in your school. Staff pulling together as a community makes work to improve school culture sustainable and authentic.

I repeat: What happens *now?*

Perhaps you are reading this book even though you do not have any educators of color in your school. If so, consider how you might apply these principles to preemptively make your school a culturally affirming institution that not only supports and retains educators of color but has the reputation of a place where educators of color invite their friends to apply for positions.

If you have educators of color on your faculty or staff, my hope is that you have already begun the task of applying the six principles to your work. As you do so, I encourage you to reflect on your journey and share your efforts with others. Consider journaling or even joining a national or local organization to exchange ideas and resources related to supporting and retaining educators of color.

If you have not yet begun the process of applying the six principles, it is not too late! I encourage you to return to Chapter 3 and compile data to generate an action plan. Then revisit Chapters 4–6 to identify specific strategies aligned to your goals. You will find that focusing your efforts on advancing cultural responsiveness and inclusion can lead to organizational—and personal—transformation.

Reflection Questions

1. Have you ever participated in equity training? What was your experience?
2. Is equity training currently a component of your school's orientation or professional development model? If so, to what extent does training address the "historical, social, organizational, and interpersonal dimensions of intersectional inequalities"? To what extent does training influence how educators teach and interact with students and colleagues on a daily basis?
3. Have you ever participated in a racial affinity group? What was your experience? If you are currently involved in a racial affinity group, how does your involvement influence your work as an instructional leader? If you are not currently in a group, how might involvement in a racial affinity group influence your work?

4. Visit https://liberatedgenius.com/educators-racial-affinity-directory and explore registered racial affinity groups in your area. What groups did you encounter? How might you communicate your findings to educators of color in your school? What possibilities do these groups raise for your staff?
5. What steps can you take to use the strategies offered in this chapter (equity training and racial affinity groups) to lead for an inclusive community and positively influence cross-racial staff dynamics in your building?

Beyond the Text: Resources to Level Up

Buckner, L. (2021). *Cultivating and applying race equity mindsets among K–12 education leaders: Key questions for reflection.* WestEd. https://files.eric.ed.gov/fulltext/ED616061.pdf

Great Schools Partnership. (n.d.). *Racial affinity groups: Guide for school leaders.* https://www.greatschoolspartnership.org/resources/educational-equity/racial-affinity-groups-guide-for-school-leaders/

Illinois State Board of Education. (n.d.). *Diversity equity and inclusion provider evaluation tool.* https://www.isbe.net/Documents/DEI-Tool-2021-2022.pdf

National Equity Project. (n.d.). Resources. https://www.nationalequityproject.org/resources

Racial Equity Tools. (n.d.). Home page. http://www.racialequitytools.org

APPENDIX A:
Social Identity Reflection Tool

Directions: Using the spaces below, describe your identity related to each social construct. Reflect on the level of access, privilege, and advantage linked with each identity marker.

Ethnicity	Race	Gender
Gender expression	Sex	Sexual orientation
Nationality	Education level	Social class
Citizenship	First language	Ability
Body (physical shape)	Hair and hair texture	Religion
Age	Neurodiversity	Mental health

Now read the following excerpt from poet and activist Audre Lorde's (2012; capitalization as in original text) essay "Age, Race, Class, and Sex: Women Redefining Difference" and consider the following questions:

- What is the "mythical norm" to which Lorde refers?
- How do our assumptions about what constitutes "normal" obscure our understanding of power?

Somewhere, on the edge of consciousness, there is what I call a *mythical norm*, which each one of us within our hearts knows "that is not me." In america, this norm is usually defined as white, thin, male, young, heterosexual, christian, and financially secure. It is with this mythical norm that the trappings of power reside within this society. Those of us who stand outside that power often identify one way in which we are different, and we assume that to be the primary cause of all oppression, forgetting other distortions around difference, some of which we ourselves may be practising. (p. 116)

APPENDIX B:

Guiding Principles for Effective Pulse Meetings

Pulse meetings are carefully structured and planned even before the initial encounter. Here are some guiding principles for an effective pulse meeting.

Before

Announce	Generate Plan	Determine Logistics	Create Agenda
Communicate to staff regarding the what, when, and why of pulse meetings.	Identify whom you want to meet with. Plan topics and script questions prior to the meeting.	Develop a plan to meet at a day, time, and location convenient for the teacher. Set up space in advance to facilitate one-to-one conversations.	Develop a loose guide to pace discussion. Use a similar agenda across meetings for continuity. Script questions and approximate time stamps for discussing each topic.

(continued)

(continued)

During

Honor Time	Frame Purpose	Reinforce Norms	Actively Listen
Respect the educator's time by sticking to your time commitment (start and end on time). Verbally convey thanks for agreeing to meet and share their experiences.	Begin meeting by restating the purpose of pulse meetings: to center teacher voices and experiences and gather recommendations to improve organizational conditions.	Restate norms of confidentiality and safety. Explain plan to ensure confidentiality and who will be privy to information shared.	Face speaker and maintain eye contact. Minimize talk time. More than 80 percent of talk time should come from the teacher. Paraphrase or summarize key ideas to confirm comprehension when appropriate.
Take Notes	**Ask Questions**	**Note Nonverbals**	**Be Accountable**
Ask permission to take notes to accurately capture ideas.	When appropriate, pose questions to deepen understanding, ask for examples, or request clarification.	Pay attention to signs of (dis)comfort conveyed by body language.	Withhold judgment and unsolicited advice. Take responsibility when needed (no deflections or rationalizing).

After

Convey Thanks	Communicate Timeline	Reflect on Themes
Reiterate gratitude for sharing time and experiences. Follow up with appropriate compensation or reciprocity.	Explain next steps (e.g., collection of additional data, reflection, development of action plan). Communicate tentative timeline to share learnings.	After each pulse meeting, maintain a record of takeaways, questions, or new insights. Schedule time to synthesize learnings from across all meetings.

APPENDIX C:
Sample Topics and Questions for Pulse Meetings

School Vision and Mission

- Can you tell me about what shaped your decision to become a teacher?
- What influenced you to teach here? What attracted you to your current position at our school?
- What are your thoughts about our school vision? What parts do you find compelling? Do you perceive our efforts as supporting all students and school community members in accomplishing that vision? In what areas do we fall short?
- Consider the symbols and artifacts of this school (e.g., mascot). To what extent do you feel these symbols are inclusive and welcoming to everyone?

Leadership and Staff Culture

- What, if anything, do you look forward to most when you come to work? What do you like least about working here?
- If I gave you a magic wand to change anything about working here, what would you change? How would this change add to your satisfaction?
- Do you feel you are a valued asset to our school? If so, what things contribute to this feeling? If not, what can be done differently for you to feel like a valued and important member of this community?

- Do you feel like you are recognized for your efforts and achievements?
- How do you like to be recognized? What is meaningful for you? What is not meaningful for you?
- From your vantage point, how would you describe the culture of and relationships in the school? What policies, procedures, or practices can be implemented to improve school culture and relationships?
- Have you ever had the opportunity to receive mentoring—either formal or informal—in our school? How would you describe the relationship? To what extent, if any, did it positively contribute to your experience as a teacher in our building?
- Where do you see yourself professionally in a year? Five years? Ten years? To what extent, if any, can we support you in these aspirations?
- Are there any existing leadership opportunities that you are interested in? Have you experienced any barriers or obstacles to pursuing these leadership opportunities?
- Are there any leadership opportunities that do not currently exist that you think would be beneficial to our students and community?
- Based on your personal experiences and observations, what can be done to better support and retain educators of color in our building?
- Would you recommend our school to friends or colleagues looking for a job? Why or why not?

Instructional Culture

- As a classroom teacher, what impact do you hope to make on your students? What resources, tools, or support can help you achieve these goals? How satisfied are you with the current resources, tools, and support you receive?
- Do you feel like your talents, interests, and skills are recognized and leveraged in your work as a teacher? What can be done so you can incorporate those into your work and increase your influence on our school community?
- What types of professional development and support have you experienced? What has been helpful in your development? What has been least helpful? What is missing?

- What would you like to learn more about as it relates to your discipline and/or teaching?
- Tell me about the type of feedback you are receiving. To what extent is the feedback clear, rooted in evidence, and actionable? What is working for you? What is not working for you? What recommendations do you have to improve our processes related to feedback?
- From your vantage point, do the day-to-day expectations and demands allow for work–life balance? What policies, procedures, or practices can be created or modified to allow for greater flexibility and work–life balance?

Turnover

- Have you ever considered leaving? What factor(s) influenced you to stay?
- What might influence you to leave?

APPENDIX D:
Pulse Meeting Agenda

Using the principles for effective pulse meetings and sample topic and questions from Appendices B and C, generate an agenda with guiding questions for an upcoming pulse meeting.

Pulse Meeting Agenda Template

Opening/Purpose ____ min	
Topic 1 ____ min	
Topic 2 ____ min	
Topic 3 ____ min	
Closing ____ min	
Next Steps ____ min	

References

Achinstein, B., & Ogawa, R. T. (2012). New teachers of color and culturally responsive teaching in an era of educational accountability: Caught in a double bind. *Journal of Educational Change, 13*(1), 1–39.

Achinstein, B., Ogawa, R. T., Sexton, D., & Freitas, C. (2010). Retaining teachers of color: A pressing problem and a potential strategy for "hard-to-staff" schools. *Review of Educational Research, 80*(1), 71–107.

Aguirre, J. M., & Zavala, M. (2013). Making culturally responsive mathematics teaching explicit: A lesson analysis tool. *Pedagogies: An International Journal, 8*(2), 163–190.

Allen, K.-A., Kern, M. L., Vella-Brodrick, D., & Waters, L. (2018). Understanding the priorities of Australian secondary schools through an analysis of their mission and vision statements. *Educational Administration Quarterly, 54*(2), 249–274.

Allen, K.-A., & Kern, P. (2018, June 14). School vision and mission statements should not be dismissed as empty words. *The Conversation.* https://theconversation.com/school-vision-and-mission-statements-should-not-be-dismissed-as-empty-words-97375

Almeida, D. (1997). The hidden half: A history of Native American women's education. *Harvard Educational Review, 67*(4): 757–772.

Amos, Y. T. (2020). "Are you gonna take my job away?": Latina bilingual education teachers' relationships with white colleagues in a white racial frame. *Urban Education, 55*(4), 640–666.

Anderson, J. D. (1988). *The education of Blacks in the South, 1860–1935.* University of North Carolina Press.

Anderson, M. D. (2015, August 6). Why schools need more teachers of color—For white students. *The Atlantic.* https://www.theatlantic.com/education/archive/2015/08/teachers-of-color-white-students/400553/

Aronson, B., & Laughter, J. (2016). The theory and practice of culturally relevant education: A synthesis of research across content areas. *Review of Educational Research, 86*(1), 163–206.

Aronson, B., & Laughter, J. (2020). The theory and practice of culturally relevant education: Expanding the conversation to include gender and sexuality equity. *Gender and Education, 32*(2), 262–279.

Au, K. H.-P. (1980). Participation structures in a reading lesson with Hawaiian children: Analysis of a culturally appropriate instructional event. *Anthropology & Education Quarterly, 11*(2), 91–115.

Baker, B. D., & Green, P. C. (2014). Conceptions of equity and adequacy in school finance. In H. F. Ladd & M. E. Goertz (Eds.), *Handbook of research in education finance and policy* (pp. 231–243). Routledge.

Barlow, R. (2014, January 16). BU research: A riddle reveals depth of gender bias. *BU Today*. https://www.bu.edu/articles/2014/bu-research-riddle-reveals-the-depth-of-gender-bias/

Bartanen, B., & Grissom, J. (2019). *School principal race and the hiring and retention of racially diverse teachers*. (EdWorkingPaper No. 19-59). Annenberg Institute, Brown University.

Bednar, S., & Gicheva, D. (2019). Workplace support and diversity in the market for public school teachers. *Education Finance and Policy, 14*(2), 272–297.

Belle, D., Tartarilla, A. B., Wapman, M., Schlieber, M., & Mercurio, A. E. (2021). "I can't operate, that boy is my son!": Gender schemas and a classic riddle. *Sex Roles, 85*, 161–171.

Bendick, M., Jr., Egan, M. L., & Lofhjelm, S. M. (2001). Workforce diversity training: From anti-discrimination compliance to organizational development. *Human Resource Planning, 24*(2), 10–25.

Benson, T., & Fiarman, S. (n.d.). Evaluating equity training: 3 tips for optimizing antiracist teacher PD [Blog post]. *KickUp*. https://www.kickup.co/blog/evaluating-equity-training-optimizing-antiracist-teacher-pd

Berry, B., Montgomery, D., & Snyder, J. (2008). *Urban teacher residency models and institutes of higher education: Implications for teacher preparation*. (ED503644). Center for Teaching Quality.

Bezrukova, K., Spell, C. S., Perry, J. L., & Jehn, K. A. (2016). A meta-analytical integration of over 40 years of research on diversity training evaluation. *Psychological Bulletin, 142*(11), 1227–1274.

Blackwell, K. (2018, August 9). Why people of color need spaces without white people. *The Arrow*. https://arrow-journal.org/why-people-of-color-need-spaces-without-white-people/

Blase, J., & Blase, J. (1998). *Handbook of instructional leadership: How really good principals promote teaching and learning*. Corwin Press.

Blase, J., & Blase, J. (2000). Effective instructional leadership: Teachers' perspectives on how principals promote teaching and learning in schools. *Journal of Educational Administration, 38*(2), 130–141.

Blase, J., Blase, J., & Du, F. (2008). The mistreated teacher: A national study. *Journal of Educational Administration, 46*(3), 263–301.

Blazar, D. (2021). *Teachers of color, culturally responsive teaching, and student outcomes: Experimental evidence from the random assignment of teachers to classes.* (EdWorkingPaper No. 21-501). Annenberg Institute, Brown University.

Blitz, L. V., & Kohl, B. G., Jr. (2012). Addressing racism in the organization: The role of white racial affinity groups in creating change. *Administration in Social Work, 36*(5), 479–498.

Boud, D., Keogh, R., & Walker, D. (2013). Promoting reflection in learning: A model. In *Reflection: Turning experience into learning* (pp. 18–40). Routledge.

Bridwell, S. D. (2012). School leadership: Lessons from the lived experiences of urban educators. *Journal of Ethnographic & Qualitative Research, 7*(2), 52–63.

Bristol, T. J. (2018). To be alone or in a group: An exploration into how the school-based experiences differ for Black male teachers across one urban school district. *Urban Education, 53*(3), 334–354.

Bristol, T. J., & Mentor, M. (2018). Policing and teaching: The positioning of Black male teachers as agents in the universal carceral apparatus. *The Urban Review, 50*(2), 218–234.

Bristol, T. J., Wallace, D. J., Manchanda, S., & Rodriguez, A. (2020). Supporting Black male preservice teachers: Evidence from an alternative teacher certification program. *Peabody Journal of Education, 95*(5), 484–497.

Brockenbrough, E. (2015). "The discipline stop": Black male teachers and the politics of urban school discipline. *Education and Urban Society, 47*(5), 499–522.

Brown, K. M., & Wynn, S. R. (2007). Teacher retention issues: How some principals are supporting and keeping new teachers. *Journal of School Leadership, 17*(6), 664–698.

Bui, Y. N., & Fagan, Y. M. (2013). The effects of an integrated reading comprehension strategy: A culturally responsive teaching approach for fifth-grade students' reading comprehension. *Preventing School Failure, 57*(2), 59–69.

Campoli, A. K., & Conrad-Popova, D. (2017). Invisible threads: Working conditions, interpersonal relationships, and turnover among Black female teachers. In A. Farinde-Wu, A. Allen-Handy, & C. W. Lewis (Eds.), *Black female teachers* (Vol. 6, pp. 117–134). Emerald Publishing.

Cardwell, M. (1996). *Dictionary of psychology.* Fitzroy Dearborn.

Carey, R. L. (2020). Missing misters: Uncovering the pedagogies and positionalities of male teachers of color in the school lives of Black and Latino adolescent boys. *Race Ethnicity and Education, 23*(3), 392–413.

Carter, P. L., & Welner, K. G. (Eds.). (2013). *Closing the opportunity gap: What America must do to give every child an even chance.* Oxford University Press.

Carter Andrews, D. J., Castro, E., Cho, C. L., Petchauer, E., Richmond, G., & Floden, R. (2019). Changing the narrative on diversifying the teaching workforce: A look at historical and contemporary factors that inform recruitment and retention of teachers of color. *Journal of Teacher Education, 70*(1), 6–12.

Carvalho-Grevious, M. J., & Ford Sabbath, T. (2018). Uniting macro and micro practice enhances diversity training. *Reflections: Narratives of Professional Helping, 23*(4), 67–75. https://reflectionsnarrativesofprofessionalhelping.org/index.php/Reflections/article/view/1517

Carver-Thomas, D. (2017). *Diversifying the field: Barriers to recruiting and retaining teachers of color and how to overcome them. Literature review.* (ED582730). Equity Assistance Center Region II, Intercultural Development Research Association.

Carver-Thomas, D. (2018). *Diversifying the teaching profession: How to recruit and retain teachers of color.* Learning Policy Institute.

Carver-Thomas, D., & Darling-Hammond, L. (2017a). *Teacher turnover: Why it matters and what we can do about it.* Learning Policy Institute.

Carver-Thomas, D., & Darling-Hammond, L. (2017b). Why Black women teachers leave and what can be done about it. In A. Farinde-Wu, A. Allen-Handy, & C. W. Lewis (Eds.), *Black female teachers* (Vol. 6, pp. 159–184). Emerald Publishing.

Cavazos, V. (2021, December 9). KOLD investigates: Tucson Unified teacher on administrative leave after using N-word in classroom. *KOLD News.* https://www.kold.com/2021/12/10/kold-investigates-tucson-unified-teacher-administrative-leave-after-using-n-word-classroom/

Cheng, S., Corrington, A., Dinh, J. V., Hebl, M., King, E., Ng, L., Reyes, D. L., Salas, E., & Traylor, A. (2019). Challenging diversity training myths: Changing the conversation about diversity training to shape science and practice. *Organizational Dynamics, 48*(4), 100678.

Cherng, H.-Y. S., & Davis, L. A. (2017). Multicultural matters: An investigation of key assumptions of multicultural education reform in teacher education. *Journal of Teacher Education, 70*(3), 219–236.

Cherng, H.-Y. S., & Halpin, P. F. (2016). The importance of minority teachers: Student perceptions of minority versus white teachers. *Educational Researcher, 45*(7), 407–420.

Choi, Y. (2013). Teaching social studies for newcomer English language learners: Toward culturally relevant pedagogy. *Multicultural Perspectives, 15*(1), 12–18.

Civil, M., & Khan, L. H. (2001). Mathematics instruction developed from a garden theme. *Teaching Children Mathematics, 7*(7), 400–405.

Cohen, A. S. (2016, March–April). Harvard's eugenics era. *Harvard Magazine.* https://www.harvardmagazine.com/2016/03/harvards-eugenics-era.

Cole, B. (2019, May 31). New York teacher made Black students act as slaves in mock auction, told them to call white students playing owners 'master'. *Newsweek.* https://www.newsweek.com/new-york-teacher-made-black-students-act-slaves-mock-auction-told-them-call-1440377

Cullen, M. (2008). *35 dumb things well-intended people say: Surprising things we say that widen the diversity gap.* Wordclay.

Curry-Stevens, A., & Lopezrevoredo, A. (2015). *Learning from educators of color: Licensed but not teaching in Oregon's public schools.* Center to Advance Racial Equity, Portland State University.

DeAngelis, T. (2015). In search of cultural competence. *Monitor on Psychology, 46*(3), 64. https://www.apa.org/monitor/2015/03/cultural-competence

Decker, D. M., Dona, D. P., & Christenson, S. L. (2007). Behaviorally at-risk African American students: The importance of student–teacher relationships for student outcomes. *Journal of School Psychology, 45*(1), 83–109.

Dee, T. S. (2004). Teachers, race, and student achievement in a randomized experiment. *The Review of Economics and Statistics, 86*(1), 195–210.

Delpit, L. (1988). The silenced dialogue: Power and pedagogy in educating other people's children. *Harvard Educational Review, 58*(3), 280–299.

Denboba, D. (1993). *MCHB/DSCSHCN guidance for competitive applications, maternal and child health improvement projects for children with special health care needs.* U.S. Department of Health and Human Services, Health Services and Resources Administration.

Detert, J. R., Burris, E. R., & Harrison, D. A. (2010). Debunking four myths about employee silence. *Harvard Business Review, 88*(6), 26.

Diamond, J. B., Randolph, A., & Spillane, J. P. (2004). Teachers' expectations and sense of responsibility for student learning: The importance of race, class, and organizational habitus. *Anthropology & Education Quarterly, 35*(1), 75–98.

Dixon, D., Griffin, A., & Teoh, M. (2019). *If you listen, we will stay: Why teachers of color leave and how to disrupt teacher turnover.* (ED603193). The Education Trust.

Dixson, A. D., & Dingus, J. E. (2008). In search of our mothers' gardens: Black women teachers and professional socialization. *Teachers College Record, 110*(4), 805–837.

Donato, R., & Hanson, J. (2012). Legally white, socially "Mexican": The politics of de jure and de facto school segregation in the American Southwest. *Harvard Educational Review, 82*(2), 202–225.

Duncan-Andrade, J. (2007). Gangstas, wankstas, and ridas: Defining, developing, and supporting effective teachers in urban schools. *International Journal of Qualitative Studies in Education, 20*(6), 617–638.

El-Amin, A., Seider, S., Graves, D., Tamerat, J., Clark, S., Soutter, M., Johannsen, J., & Malhotra, S. (2017). Critical consciousness: A key to student achievement. *Phi Delta Kappan, 98*(5), 18–23. https://kappanonline.org/critical-consciousness-key-student-achievement/

El-Mekki, S. (2020). *Respecting educator activists of color: The anti-racist guide to teacher retention.* Center for Black Educator Development. https://www.thecenterblacked.org/s/CBED21-A2E-Retention-Toolkit-012.pdf

El-Mekki, S. (2022, April 20). Recruiting Black teachers into a burning schoolhouse won't help to retain them [Blog post]. *Philly's 7th Ward.* https://phillys7thward.org/2022/04/recruiting-black-teachers-into-a-burning-schoolhouse-wont-help-to-retain-them/

Ensign, J. (2003). Including culturally relevant math in an urban school. *Educational Studies, 34*(4), 414–423.

Escalante, J., & Dirmann, J. (1990). The Jaime Escalante Math Program. (ED345942; reprinted from *The Journal of Negro Education, 59*[3], 407–423). http://files.eric.ed.gov/fulltext/ED345942.pdf

Eurich, T. (2018). What self-awareness really is (and how to cultivate it). *Harvard Business Review.* https://hbr.org/2018/01/what-self-awareness-really-is-and-how-to-cultivate-it

Fairclough, A. (2004). The costs of *Brown:* Black teachers and school integration. *The Journal of American History, 91*(1), 43–55.

Farinde, A. A., Allen, A., & Lewis, C. W. (2016). Retaining Black teachers: An examination of Black female teachers' intentions to remain in K–12 classrooms. *Equity & Excellence in Education, 49*(1), 115–127.

Farinde-Wu, A., Allen-Handy, A., Butler, B. R., & Lewis, C. W. (2017). The urban factor: Examining why Black female educators teach in under-resourced, urban schools. In A. Farinde-Wu, A. Allen-Handy, & C. W. Lewis (Eds.), *Black female teachers* (Vol. 6, 73–92). Emerald Publishing.

Farkas, G., Grobe, R. P., Sheehan, D., & Shuan, Y. (1990). Cultural resources and school success: Gender, ethnicity, and poverty groups within an urban school district. *American Sociological Review, 55*(1), 127–142.

Fergus, E. (2017). Confronting colorblindness. *Phi Delta Kappan, 98*(5), 30–35. https://kappanonline.org/confronting-colorblindness/

Fergus, E. (2019). Confronting our beliefs about poverty and discipline. *Phi Delta Kappan, 100*(5), 31–34.

Ferguson, R. F. (2003). Teachers' perceptions and expectations and the Black–white test score gap. *Urban Education, 38*(4), 460–507.

Ferlazzo, L. (2015, January 6). Response: The teachers of color "disappearance crisis." *Education Week.* https://www.edweek.org/leadership/opinion-response-the-teachers-of-color-disappearance-crisis/2015/01

Ferlazzo, L. (2019, September 11). Author interview with Dr. Gholdy Muhammad: "If we 'don't see race,' we don't see 'students' magic.'" *Education Week.* https://www.edweek.org/teaching-learning/opinion-if-we-dont-see-race-we-dont-see-students-magic/2019/09

Ferlazzo, L. (2020, January 28). Author interview with Dr. Gholdy Muhammad: "Cultivating genius." *Education Week.* https://www.edweek.org/teaching-learning/opinion-author-interview-with-dr-gholdy-muhammad-cultivating-genius/2020/01

Flores, G. M. (2011). Racialized tokens: Latina teachers negotiating, surviving and thriving in a white woman's profession. *Qualitative Sociology, 34*(2), 313–335.

Foster, M. (1993). Educating for competence in community and culture: Exploring the views of exemplary African-American teachers. *Urban Education, 27*(4), 370–394.

Foster, M. (1995). *African American teachers and culturally relevant pedagogy.* (ED382726). ERIC.

Freire, P. (1970). *Pedagogy of the oppressed.* Seabury Press.

Gabbadon, A. T. (2022). *"Not backing down": A narrative inquiry of Black women teachers in urban schools* (Doctoral dissertation, Temple University). Retrieved from Temple University Libraries. https://scholarshare.temple.edu/handle/20.500.12613/7728

Gándara, P., & Orfield, G. (2010). *A return to the "Mexican room": The segregation of Arizona's English learners.* The Civil Rights Project/Proyecto Derechos Civiles. https://civilrightsproject.ucla.edu/research/k-12-education/language-minority-students/a-return-to-the-mexican-room-the-segregation-of-arizonas-english-learners-1

García-Nevarez, A. G., Stafford, M. E., & Arias, B. (2005). Arizona elementary teachers' attitudes toward English language learners and the use of Spanish in classroom instruction. *Bilingual Research Journal, 29*(2), 295–317.

Gardenswartz, L., & Rowe, A. (1997). Diversity Q & A: Effectively moving beyond affirmative action with a diversity task force. *Mosaics, SHRM Focuses on Workplace Diversity, 3*(5).

Gay, G. (2002). Preparing for culturally responsive teaching. *Journal of Teacher Education, 53*(2), 106–116.

Gay, G. (2010). *Culturally responsive teaching: Theory, research, and practice* (2nd ed.). Teachers College Press.

Georgetown University Center for Child and Human Development. (n.d.). *Curricula enhancement module series: Definitions of cultural competence.* https://nccc.georgetown.edu/curricula/culturalcompetence.html

Gere, A. R. (2005). Indian heart/white man's head: Native-American teachers in Indian schools, 1880–1930. *History of Education Quarterly, 45*(1), 38–65.

Gershenson, S., Holt, S. B., & Papageorge, N. W. (2016). Who believes in me? The effect of student–teacher demographic match on teacher expectations. *Economics of Education Review, 52,* 209–224.

Gino, F., & Coffman, K. (2021, September–October). Unconscious bias training that works. *Harvard Business Review.* https://hbr.org/2021/09/unconscious-bias-training-that-works

Gist, C. D., & Bristol, T. J. (Eds.). (2022). *Handbook of research on teachers of color and Indigenous teachers.* American Educational Research Association.

Givens, J. R. (2021). *Fugitive pedagogy: Carter G. Woodson and the art of Black teaching.* Harvard University Press.

Gordon, J. A. (1997). Teachers of color speak to issues of respect and image. *The Urban Review, 29*(1), 41–66.

Gorski, P. (2012). Equity and social justice from the inside-out: Ten commitments for intercultural educators. In N. Palaiologou & G. Dietz (Eds.), *Mapping the broad* field of multicultural and intercultural education worldwide: Towards the development of a new citizen* (pp. 388–401). Cambridge Scholars Publishers.

Griffin, A. (2018). *Our stories, our struggles, our strengths: Perspectives and reflections from Latino teachers.* (ED588864). The Education Trust.

Grissom, J. A., Rodriguez, L. A., & Kern, E. C. (2017). Teacher and principal diversity and the representation of students of color in gifted programs: Evidence from national data. *The Elementary School Journal, 117*(3), 396–422.

Grooms, A. A., Mahatmya, D., & Johnson, E. T. (2021). The retention of educators of color amidst institutionalized racism. *Educational Policy, 35*(2), 180–212.

Guilfoyle, B. M. (2015). Colorblind ideology expressed through children's picture books: A social justice issue. *Jesuit Higher Education: A Journal, 4*(2), 37–56.

Guy, S. (2019). What research tells us about diversity training. *SWE: Magazine of the Society of Women Engineers, 65*(2), 52–58. https://docplayer.net/144823245-What-motivates-men-to-champion-gender-diversity.html

Hammond, Z. (2015). *Culturally responsive teaching and the brain: Promoting authentic engagement and rigor among culturally and linguistically diverse students.* Corwin.

Harris, J. I., Winskowski, A. M., & Engdahl, B. E. (2007). Types of workplace social support in the prediction of job satisfaction. *The Career Development Quarterly, 56*(2), 150–156.

Hess, F. M., & Leal, D. L. (1997). Minority teachers, minority students, and college matriculation: A new look at the role-modeling hypothesis. *Policy Studies Journal, 25*(2), 235–248.

Hubert, T. L. (2014). Learners of mathematics: High school students' perspectives of culturally relevant mathematics pedagogy. *Journal of African American Studies, 18*(3), 324–336.

Illinois State Board of Education (ISBE). (n.d.). *Diversity equity and inclusion provider evaluation tool.* https://www.isbe.net/Documents/DEI-Tool-2021-2022.pdf

In top ten of science teachers. (1995, February 9). *Buffalo Reporter.* https://www.buffalo.edu/ubreporter/archive/vol26/vol26n16/25.txt

Ingersoll, R. M. (2009). *Who controls teachers' work?: Power and accountability in America's schools.* Harvard University Press.

Ingersoll, R. M., & Connor, R. (2009, April). *What the national data tell us about minority and Black teacher turnover.* Paper presented at the annual meeting of the American Educational Research Association, San Diego, CA.

Ingersoll, R., & May, H. (2011). *Recruitment, retention and the minority teacher shortage.* (CPRE Research Report #RR-69). Consortium for Policy Research in Education.

Ingersoll, R., May, H., Collins, G., & Fletcher, T. (2021). Trends in the recruitment, employment and retention of teachers from under-represented racial-ethnic groups, 1987 to 2016. In C. D. Gist & T. J. Bristol (Eds.), *Handbook of research on teachers of color and Indigenous teachers* (pp. 823–840). American Educational Research Association.

Ingersoll, R. M., Merrill, E., Stuckey, D., & Collins, G. (2018). *Seven trends: The transformation of the teaching force—Updated October 2018.* (CPRE Research Report #RR 2018-2). Consortium for Policy Research in Education.

Institute for Teachers of Color Committed to Racial Justice. (n.d.). 2022–2023 Institute for Teachers of Color Committed to Racial Justice. http://www.instituteforteachersofcolor.org/2022-23-itoc.html

Jackson, R. R. (2021, April 1). The most powerful tool in a principal's arsenal. *Educational Leadership, 78*(7). https://www.ascd.org/el/articles/the-most-powerful-tool-in-a-principals-arsenal

Jacoby-Senghor, D. S., Sinclair, S., & Shelton, J. N. (2016). A lesson in bias: The relationship between implicit racial bias and performance in pedagogical contexts. *Journal of Experimental Social Psychology, 63,* 50–55.

Jones, T., & Norwood, K. J. (2017). Aggressive encounters & white fragility: Deconstructing the trope of the angry Black woman. *Iowa Law Review, 102*(5).

Juneau, S. (2001). *A history and foundation of American Indian education policy.* (ED456945). Montana State Office of Public Instruction.

Kelly, H. (2007). Racial tokenism in the school workplace: An exploratory study of Black teachers in overwhelmingly white schools. *Educational Studies, 41*(3), 230–254.

Khalifa, M. A., Gooden, M. A., & Davis, J. E. (2016). Culturally responsive school leadership: A synthesis of the literature. *Review of Educational Research, 86*(4), 1272–1311.

Kimberlé Crenshaw on intersectionality, more than two decades later. (2017, June 8). *Columbia Law School.* https://www.law.columbia.edu/news/archive/kimberle-crenshaw-intersectionality-more-two-decades-later

Kirwan Institute for the Study of Race and Ethnicity. (n.d.). *Implicit bias module series.* https://kirwaninstitute.osu.edu/implicit-bias-training

Kohli, R. (2018). Behind school doors: The impact of hostile racial climates on urban teachers of color. *Urban Education, 53*(3), 307–333.

Kohli, R. (2019). Lessons for teacher education: The role of critical professional development in teacher of color retention. *Journal of Teacher Education, 70*(1), 39–50.

Kohli, R. (2021). *Teachers of color: Resisting racism and reclaiming education.* Harvard Education Press.

Kohli, R., & Pizarro, M. (2016). Fighting to educate our own: Teachers of color, relational accountability, and the struggle for racial justice. *Equity & Excellence in Education, 49*(1), 72–84.

Kohli, R., Pizarro, M., Garcia, L. G., Kelly, L., Espinoza, M., & Cordova, J. (2021). Critical professional development and the racial justice leadership possibilities of teachers of colour in K–12 schools. *Professional Development in Education, 47*(1), 89–101.

Krasilnikova, M. B., & Sevastyanova, S. K. (2015). The issue of modern approaches to the definition of "culture." *Observatory of Culture, 4,* 98–103.

Kruger, J., & Dunning, D. (1999). Unskilled and unaware of it: How difficulties in recognizing one's own incompetence lead to inflated self-assessments. *Journal of Personality and Social Psychology, 77*(6), 1121–1134.

Kumagai, A. K., & Lypson, M. L. (2009). Beyond cultural competence: Critical consciousness, social justice, and multicultural education. *Academic Medicine, 84*(6), 782–787.

Ladson-Billings, G. (1994). *The dreamkeepers: Successful teachers of African American children.* Jossey-Bass Publishers.

Ladson-Billings, G. (1995). But that's just good teaching! The case for culturally relevant pedagogy. *Theory into Practice, 34*(3), 159–165.

Ladson-Billings, G. (2006). From the achievement gap to the education debt: Understanding achievement in U.S. schools. *Educational Researcher, 35*(7), 3–12.

Laker, B. (2022, January 10). *3 ways listening to employee feedback can contribute to business growth.* Forbes. https://www.forbes.com/sites/benjaminlaker/2022/01/10/3-ways-listening-to-employee-feedback-can-contribute-to-business-growth/

Langlie, M. L. (2008). *The effect of culturally relevant pedagogy on the mathematics achievement of Black and Hispanic high school students* (Doctoral dissertation, Northeastern University). Retrieved from Digital Repository Service, Northeastern University Library. http://hdl.handle.net/2047/d10016028

Lee, S. J. (1994). Behind the model-minority stereotype: Voices of high- and low-achieving Asian American students. *Anthropology & Education Quarterly, 25*(4), 413–429.

Lees, A., Vélez, V., & Laman, T. T. (2021). Recognition and resistance of settler colonialism in early childhood education: Perspectives and implications for Black, Indigenous, and teachers of color. *International Journal of Qualitative Studies in Education.* https://doi.org/10.1080/09518398.2021.1891319

Lindsay, C. A., & Hart, C. M. D. (2017). Exposure to same-race teachers and student disciplinary outcomes for Black students in North Carolina. *Educational Evaluation and Policy Analysis, 39*(3), 485–510.

Lipman, P. (2011). *The new political economy of urban education: Neoliberalism, race, and the right to the city.* Routledge.

Lorde, A. (2012). *Sister outsider: Essays and speeches.* Crossing Press.

Love, B. L. (2019). *We want to do more than survive: Abolitionist teaching and the pursuit of educational freedom.* Beacon Press.

Lutz, M. (2017). The hidden cost of *Brown v. Board:* African American educators' resistance to desegregating schools. *Online Journal of Rural Research & Policy, 12*(4).

Mann, H. (1848). Twelfth annual report to the Massachusetts State Board of Education. In M. Mann (Ed.), *Life and works of Horace Mann* (Vol. 3, p. 669). https://www.bartleby.com/73/498.html

Marzano, R. J. (2003). *What works in schools: Translating research into action.* Association for Supervision and Curriculum Development.

Mason, S., Cole-Malott, D.-M., Teoh, M., Ravenell, A., El-Mekki, S., Seaton, K., & Woldeyohannes, M. (2021). *To be who we are: Black teachers on creating affirming school cultures.* Teach Plus and Center for Black Educator Development.

McIntosh, P. (1990). *White privilege: Unpacking the invisible knapsack.* The Legislative Library of the Northwest Territories. https://www.jstor.org/stable/community.30714426

Michael, A., & Conger, M. C. (2009). Becoming an anti-racist white ally: How a white affinity group can help. *Perspectives on Urban Education, 6*(1), 56–60.

Milner, H. R., IV. (2013). Scripted and narrowed curriculum reform in urban schools. *Urban Education, 48*(2), 163–170.

Mohatt, G., & Erickson, F. (1981). Cultural differences in teaching styles in an Odawa school: A sociolinguistic approach. In H. T. Trueba, G. P. Guthrie, & K. H.-P. Au (Eds.), *Culture and the bilingual classroom: Studies in classroom ethnography* (pp. 105–119). Newbury House Publishers.

Mosely, M. (2018). The Black Teacher Project: How racial affinity professional development sustains Black teachers. *The Urban Review, 50*(2), 267–283.

Muhammad, G. (2020). *Cultivating genius: An equity framework for culturally and historically responsive literacy.* Scholastic.

Nadal, K. L., Griffin, K. E., Wong, Y., Davidoff, K. C., & Davis, L. S. (2017). The injurious relationship between racial microaggressions and physical health: Implications for social work. *Journal of Ethnic & Cultural Diversity in Social Work, 26*(1–2), 6–17.

National Center for Education Statistics. (2018). Characteristics of public school teachers who completed alternative route to certification programs. *COE Indicators.* Institute of Education Sciences, U.S. Department of Education. https://nces.ed.gov/programs/coe/indicator/tlc

National Center for Education Statistics. (2019a). *Digest of education statistics: Table 203.50: Enrollment and percentage distribution of enrollment in public elementary and secondary schools, by race/ethnicity and region: Selected year, fall 1995 through fall 2029.* Institute of Education Sciences, U.S. Department of Education. https://nces.ed.gov/programs/digest/d19/tables/dt19_203.50.asp

National Center for Education Statistics. (2019b). *Spotlight A: Characteristics of public school teachers by race/ethnicity.* Institute of Education Sciences, U.S. Department of Education. https://nces.ed.gov/programs/raceindicators/spotlight_a.asp

National Center for Education Statistics. (2020a). Characteristics of public school principals. *COE Indicators.* Institute of Education Sciences, U.S. Department of Education. https://nces.ed.gov/programs/coe/indicator/cls

National Center for Education Statistics. (2020b). *Race and ethnicity of public school teachers and their students.* (Data Point 2020-103). Institute of Education Sciences, U.S. Department of Education. https://nces.ed.gov/pubs2020/2020103/index.asp

National Center for Education Statistics. (2022). Racial/ethnic enrollment in public schools. *COE Indicators.* Institute of Education Sciences, U.S. Department of Education. https://nces.ed.gov/programs/coe/indicator/cge

National Equity Project. (n.d.). *The three A's: Alone, affinity & alliance workshop* [Virtual workshop]. https://www.nationalequityproject.org/training/racial-affinity-structures

National Equity Project. (2021). *A space to be whole: A landscape analysis of education-based racial affinity groups in the U.S.*

National Institutes of Health. (2021). *Scientific Workforce Diversity Seminar Series (SWDSS) Seminar proceedings: Is implicit bias training effective?* https://diversity.nih.gov/sites/coswd/files/images/NIH_COSWD_SWDSS_Implicit_Bias_Proceedings_508.pdf

NEA Center for Social Justice. (2021). *Racial justice in education: Terms and definitions.* National Education Association. https://www.nea.org/professional-excellence/student-engagement/tools-tips/racial-justice-education-key-terms-and

Nevarez, C., Jouganatos, S., & Wood, J. L. (2019). Benefits of teacher diversity: Leading for transformative change. *Journal of School Administration Research and Development, 4*(1), 24–34.

Newman, D. (2016, August 2). *How well does your organization use feedback loops?* Forbes. https://www.forbes.com/sites/danielnewman/2016/08/02/how-well-does-your-organization-use-feedback-loops/

Noddings, N. (1995). Care and moral education. In W. Kohli (Ed.), *Critical conversations in philosophy of education* (pp. 137–148). Routledge.

Noddings, N. (2012). The caring relation in teaching. *Oxford Review of Education, 38*(6), 771–781.

Noe-Bustamente, L., Mora, L., Lopez, M. H. (2020, August 11). About one-in-four U.S. Hispanics have heard of Latinx, but just 3% use it. *Pew Research Center.* https://www.pewresearch.org/hispanic/2020/08/11/about-one-in-four-u-s-hispanics-have-heard-of-latinx-but-just-3-use-it/

Noon, M. (2018). Pointless diversity training: Unconscious bias, new racism and agency. *Work, Employment and Society, 32*(1), 198–209.

Oakley, D., Stowell, J., & Logan, J. R. (2009). The impact of desegregation on Black teachers in the metropolis, 1970–2000. *Ethnic and Racial Studies, 32*(9), 1576–1598.

Omi, M., & Winant, H. (1988). *Racial formation in the United States.* Routledge.

Orfield, G., Frankenberg, E., Ee, J., & Kuscera, J. (2014). Brown *at 60: Great progress, a long retreat and an uncertain future.* The Civil Rights Project/Proyecto Derechos Civiles. https://www.civilrightsproject.ucla.edu/research/k-12-education/integration-and-diversity/brown-at-60-great-progress-a-long-retreat-and-an-uncertain-future

Organisation for Economic Co-operation and Development. (2018). *The future of education and skills: Education 2030.* http://www.oecd.org/education/2030/E2030%20Position%20Paper%20(05.04.2018).pdf

Pabon, A. (2016). Waiting for Black Superman: A look at a problematic assumption. *Urban Education, 51*(8), 915–939.

Paris, D., & Alim, H. S. (2014). What are we seeking to sustain through culturally sustaining pedagogy? A loving critique forward. *Harvard Educational Review, 84*(1), 85–100.

Pitts, D. W. (2007). Representative bureaucracy, ethnicity, and public schools: Examining the link between representation and performance. *Administration & Society, 39*(4), 497–526.

Pizarro, M., & Kohli, R. (2020). "I stopped sleeping": Teachers of color and the impact of racial battle fatigue. *Urban Education, 55*(7), 967–991.

Pollock, M. (2004). *Colormute: Race talk dilemmas in an American School*. Princeton University Press.

Pour-Khorshid, F. (2018). Cultivating sacred spaces: A racial affinity group approach to support critical educators of color. *Teaching Education, 29*(4), 318–329.

Project Implicit. (2011). *Ethical considerations*. https://implicit.harvard.edu/implicit/ethics.html

Quiocho, A., & Rios, F. (2000). The power of their presence: Minority group teachers and schooling. *Review of Educational Research, 70*(4), 485–528.

Ramirez, E., & Donovan, S. J. (2021). Harm and healing: Reading with an ABAR (anti-bias, antiracist) lens. *Voices from the Middle, 28*(4), 54–59.

Richardson-Gibbs, M. A., & Klein, M. D. (2014). *Making preschool inclusion work: Strategies for supporting children, teachers, & programs*. Paul H. Brookes Publishing.

Riley, R. W. (1998). Our teachers should be excellent, and they should look like America. *Education and Urban Society, 31*(1), 18–29.

Rivera-McCutchen, R. L. (2021). "We don't got time for grumbling": Toward an ethic of radical care in urban school leadership. *Educational Administration Quarterly, 57*(2), 257–289.

Robertson, R. (1988). The sociological significance of culture: Some general considerations. *Theory, Culture & Society, 5*(1), 3–23.

Rodgers, C., & Skelton, J. (2014). Professional development and mentoring in support of teacher retention. *Journal on School Educational Technology, 9*(3), 1–11.

Rodriguez, J. L., Bustamante Jones, E., Peng, V. O., & Park, C. D. (2004). Promoting academic achievement and identity development among diverse high school students. *The High School Journal, 87*(3), 44–53.

Rogo, P. (2020, October 26). Baltimore teacher fired after calling students the N-word. *Essence*. https://www.essence.com/news/baltimore-teacher-calls-students-n-word/

Rubin, D. I. (2011). The disheartened teacher: Living in the age of standardization, high-stakes assessments, and No Child Left Behind (NCLB). *Changing English, 18*(4), 407–416.

Ruhl, C. (2023, February 24). Implicit bias (unconscious bias): Definition & examples. *Simply Psychology*. https://www.simplypsychology.org/implicit-bias.html

Rury, J. L. (2012). *Education and social change: Contours in the history of American schooling*. Routledge.

Rynes, S., & Rosen, B. (1995). A field survey of factors affecting the adoption and perceived success of diversity training. *Personnel Psychology, 48*(2), 247–270.

Schaeffer, K. (2021, December 10). America's public school teachers are far less racially and ethnically diverse than their students. *Pew Research Center.* https://www.pewresearch.org/fact-tank/2021/12/10/americas-public-school-teachers-are-far-less-racially-and-ethnically-diverse-than-their-students/

Scott, K. (2020, October 27). 6 ways to roll out Radical Candor like a boss [Blog post]. *Radical Candor.* https://www.radicalcandor.com/rolling-out-radical-candor-part-one/

Singleton, G. E., & Hays, C. (2008). Beginning courageous conversations about race. In M. Pollock (Ed.), *Everyday antiracism: Getting real about race in school* (pp. 18–23). New Press.

Skiba, R. J., Fergus, E., & Gregory, A. (2022). The new Jim Crow in school 1: Exclusionary discipline and structural racism. In E. J. Sabornie & D. L. Espelage (Eds.), *Handbook of classroom management* (3rd ed., pp. 211–230). Routledge.

Slisco, A. (2021, April 13). Oklahoma teacher who called student N-word placed on administrative leave. *Newsweek.* https://www.newsweek.com/oklahoma-teacher-who-called-student-n-word-placed-administrative-leave-1583426

Sorokin, P. A. (1947). *Society, culture, and personality: Their structure and dynamics, a system of general sociology.* Harper.

Spring, J. (2016). *Deculturalization and the struggle for equality: A brief history of the education of dominated cultures in the United States* (8th ed.). Routledge.

Spring, J. (2019). *American education: An introduction to social and political aspects.* Routledge.

Staats, C. (2016). Understanding implicit bias: What educators should know. *American Educator, 39*(4), 29–33.

Stanley, D. A. (2021). "I want to leave ASAP": Black women teachers discuss the role of administrative support and teacher turnover. *Journal of School Leadership, 31*(3), 209–226.

Stanley, D. A. (2022). Blood, sweat, and tears: Black women teacher's organizational experiences in schools. *International Journal of Qualitative Studies in Education, 35*(2), 194–209.

Steensland, B. (2011). Sociology of culture. *Oxford Bibliographies.* https://www.oxfordbibliographies.com/view/document/obo-9780199756384/obo-9780199756384-0055.xml

Stevenson, H. C. (2014). *Promoting racial literacy in schools: Differences that make a difference.* Teachers College Press.

Sue, D. W. (Ed.). (2010). *Microaggressions and marginality: Manifestation, dynamics, and impact.* Wiley.

Swalwell, K. (2012). Confronting white privilege. *Teaching Tolerance, 42,* 23–26. https://www.learningforjustice.org/magazine/fall-2012/confronting-white-privilege

Tamura, E. H. (1995). Gender, schooling and teaching, and the Nisei in Hawai'i: An episode in American immigration history, 1900–1940. *Journal of American Ethnic History, 14*(4), 3–26.

Tatum, B. D. (2017). *"Why are all the Black kids sitting together in the cafeteria?" And other conversations about race* (20th anniv. ed.). Basic Books.

Texas Higher Education Coordinating Board. (n.d.). The African American struggle for civil rights: Desegregation and integration. *OERTX Repository.* https://oertx.highered.texas.gov/courseware/lesson/1407/student/?task=3

Tucker-Smith, T. N. (2021, March 1). The illusion of equity PD. *Educational Leadership, 78*(6). https://www.ascd.org/el/articles/the-illusion-of-equity-pd

U.S. Department of Housing and Urban Development. (n.d.). *DEIA definitions.* https://www.hud.gov/program_offices/administration/admabout/diversity_inclusion/definitions

Valdez, L. (1994). Pensamiento serpentino. In *Luis Valdez—Early works: Actos, Bernabé and pensameinto serpentino.* Arte Público Press.

van der Vyver, C. P., van der Westhuizen, P. C., & Meyer, L. W. (2014). Caring school leadership: A South African study. *Educational Management Administration & Leadership, 42*(1), 61–74.

Villegas, A. M., & Irvine, J. J. (2010). Diversifying the teaching force: An examination of major arguments. *The Urban Review, 42*(3), 175–192.

Villegas, A. M., & Lucas, T. (2002). Preparing culturally responsive teachers: Rethinking the curriculum. *Journal of Teacher Education, 53*(1), 20–32.

Warren-Grice, A. (2021). *A space to be whole: A landscape analysis of education-based racial affinity groups in the United States.* Black Teacher Project, National Equity Project. https://www.blackteacherproject.org/s/BTP-Landscape_Analysis_Racial_Affinity_US_2021.pdf

Watlington, E., Shockley, R., Guglielmino, P., & Felsher, R. (2010). The high cost of leaving: An analysis of the cost of teacher turnover. *Journal of Education Finance, 36*(1), 22–37.

Wortham, S., & Contreras, M. (2002). Struggling toward culturally relevant pedagogy in the Latino diaspora. *Journal of Latinos and Education, 1*(2), 133–144.

Index

The letter *f* following a page locator denotes a figure.

action, assess and plan for
    conduct prework, 51
    gather information from educators of color, 54–60, 60–66*f*
    readiness assessment, 51, 51*f*, 52–54*f*
    summary, 138
advancement
    opportunities for, 50
    programs for, 129–130
agency, redistributing, 105
American Indian/Alaska Native educators, decline in, 12, 13*f*
Asian American Pacific Islander (AAPI), 5, 10
autonomy, teacher, 49–50, 100–101

belonging. *See* inclusion
bias
    disciplinary, 48
    implicit, 30–31
    interrogating, 28–31
    meaning of, 28
    staff dynamics and, 47–48
bias training, 28–29

Black students in segregated schools, 24, 26*f*
Black teacher workforce, historically, 12

clinical experience, 71–72
collaboration, 80–81, 103–106
collegiality, critical friends model, 103–104
colorblindness, 25–27, 95–96
community, leadership for an inclusive equity training, 113–124
    racial affinity spaces, 124–137
community partnerships, 104–106
critical consciousness, 114
critical friends model, 103–104
criticality, components of, 101–102
cultural competence, 98, 114
cultural gaps, educators of color in bridging, 8
Culturally Responsive Curriculum scorecard, 101
culture, meaning of, 88
curriculum and instruction, fostering supportive environments for, 100–102

data collection
  action step of, 54–60, 60–66f
  equity training, successful, 118–119
  focus groups for, 56
  forums for, 56
  interviews, exit and stay, 56
  surveys for, 56–58, 58f
decision making, collective, 105–106
discipline, inequity in, 36–37, 48

education, barriers to culturally
  responsive approaches
    leadership assumptions, 98–99
    misunderstandings, 96–97
    standardization, 97–98
education, culturally responsive
  approaches to
    absence, significance of, 93–96
    barriers to, 96–99
    benefits of, 91–92
    culturally relevant pedagogy model, 90
    Culturally Responsive Curriculum scorecard, 101
    emergence of, 89
    leadership self-assessment, 106, 107f
    shared characteristics of, 90–91
    teaching model, 90
educator-activist, defined, 54
educator diversity, acknowledging the importance of, 6–7, 14–15, 27, 137
educators of color. *See also* racial
  affinity groups
    autonomy of, enhancing, 100
    Black teacher workforce, historically, 12
    categories included in, 5
    colorblindness, effects on, 27
    comparison by race/ethnicity, 12, 13f
    disciplining of, 36–37
    expectations for, 7, 75–76
    expertise, valuing, 100
    in film, 10–11
    historical legacy, 9–11

  instructional supports for, 70–72
  leaders of color, importance to, 45
  misconceptions, 9, 74–75
  monitoring, 100–101
  percent of workforce, 1, 10–11
  stereotypes, 75
  term usage, viii
  turnover, reasons for, 2, 13–14, 19, 27, 44, 50, 55, 72–73
  turnover statistics, 14f
educators of color, gathering
  information from
    action plan, developing an, 62
    analysis, 61
    benchmarks, 66f
    benefits of, 55
    cautions when, 55
    charting goals and tasks, 65f
    key tasks, 64f, 65f, 66f
    reflection document, 61f
    root cause analysis, 62f
    SMART goals, 63f, 65f, 66f
    strategies, 56–58
educator workforce. *See also* teachers
  comparison by race/ethnicity, 13f
  diversity in, acknowledging the importance of, 6–7, 14–15, 27, 137
  imbalance, background of the, 11–14
  Latino/x, 10–11
  percent self-identifying as white, 1, 7
  white, turnover statistics, 14f
  white women, percent of, 1, 12
educator workforce, supporting and
  retaining a diverse
    benefits of, 7–9
    instructional culture, 48–50
    leadership opportunities, 50
    reasons for, 87
    staff dynamics in, 46–48
    support and mentoring for, 49
    vision and mission statements, 43–44
environments, fostering supportive
    autonomy, enhancing, 49–50, 100–101
    benefits of, 87

environments, fostering supportive (*cont'd*)
  centering identity and criticality in, 101–102
  community partnerships, 104–106
  for curriculum and instruction, 100–102
  home–school–community collaboration, 104–105
  for input and decision making, 105–106
  reflection and learning in, 102–103
  summary, 138
  teacher capacity and resources in, 102–104
  teacher planning and collaboration, prioritizing, 103–104
equity training
  about, 113–114
  attendance requirement, 121
  benefits of, 114
  case study: disgruntled participants, 122–124
  ineffective, 115
  intent and impact gap, 114–115
  leading for inclusion through, 116–117
  purpose of, 124
equity training, successful
  actionable next steps in, 120
  components of, 115–116
  continuity and cohesion in, 120–121
  diverse representation in, 117–118
  an explicit strategy in, 117
  facilitation for, 120
  is goal-oriented, 117
  is linked to measurable outcomes, 118–119
  leadership commitment and accountability for, 121
  participant engagement opportunities in, 119
  relational trust and, 119–120
ethics of care theory, 82
exit interviews, 56

expectations
  achievement and, 11
  of educators of color, 7, 75–76

father–son riddle, 37–38
feedback loops, 77–79
focus groups, 56
forums, 56

guiding principles for effective pulse meetings, 143–144

Harvard Implicit Association Test, 30–31, 37
Hispanic, term usage, viii
Hispanic students, percent of enrolled students, 7
home–school–community collaboration, 104–105

identity and criticality, fostering supportive environments for, 101–102
identity-based mentoring, leadership, and advancement programs, 129–130
impact and intent, 31–35, 34*f*
impact and intent gap, equity training and the, 114–115
inclusion. *See also* leadership for an inclusive community
  defined, 112
  equity training for, 116–117
  teacher voices on, 110–111
Indian boarding schools, 10, 24–25
information, gathering from educators of color
  action plan, developing an, 62
  analysis, 61
  benchmarks, 66*f*
  benefits of, 55
  cautions when, 55
  charting goals and tasks, 65*f*
  key tasks, 64*f*, 65*f*, 66*f*

reflection document, 61f
root cause analysis, 62f
SMART goals, 63f, 65f, 66f
strategies, 56–58
instructional culture and a diverse
 workforce, 48–50
instructional culture readiness
 assessment, 53–54f
instructional leadership, 45
instructional rounds for instructional
 support, 79
instructional supports
 absence of, investigating reasons for,
  73–76
 disconnects in, 70
 for educators of color, 70–72
 reasons for, 70
instructional supports, sustainable and
 high-impact
 communicating school instructional
  priorities, 77
 facilitating instructional rounds, 79
 goal-oriented observation and
  feedback loops, 77–79
 minimizing interferences to planning
  time, 81
 pedagogical expertise, 76–79
 personal well-being, 81–82
 professional capacity, 79–81
 regular and scheduled collaboration,
  80–81
 summary, 138
intent and impact
 reflection on, 31–35
 scenarios, 34f
intent and impact gap, equity training
 and the, 114–115
intersectionality, 35–39
interviews, exit and stay, 56

Japanese American students, 25

language, power of, vii–viii
Latino/x, term usage, viii

Latino/x teacher workforce, 10–11
leadership, culturally affirming
 assumptions as barrier to, 98–99
 characteristics of, 105–106
 defined, 2–3
 racial affinity groups, 132–136
 readiness assessment, 52f
 self-assessment, 106, 107f
leadership, principles of culturally
 affirming
 acknowledge that educator diversity
  matters, 5, 6, 14–15, 27, 137
 assess and plan for action, 51,
  51–54f, 54–60, 60–66f, 138
 commit to sustainable and high-
  impact instructional supports,
  76–82, 138
 cultivate reflection and self-
  awareness, 137–138
 foster supportive environments, 87,
  100–106, 138
 lead for an inclusive community, 138
leadership culture
 of micromanagement, 22
 supporting and retaining a diverse
  workforce, 44–46
 teacher voices on, 20–21, 36
leadership for an inclusive community
 equity training, 113–124
 racial affinity spaces, 124–137
leadership opportunities
 for a diverse workforce, 50
 programs for, 129–130
 teacher voices on, 20–21, 32–33
leaders of color, importance to teachers
 of color, 45

mentoring and support for a diverse
 workforce, 49, 71–72, 129–130
microaggressions, 22, 23
mission statements, 43–44, 52f

observation, goal-oriented, 77–79
organizations, culturally affirming, 2

pedagogy
    culturally relevant model, 90
    culturally responsive model, 90
    experts for instructional support, 76–79
people of color, term usage, vii–viii
planning and collaboration, fostering supportive environments for, 103–104
planning time, minimizing interferences to, 81
political engagement and activism, 126–127
power, redistributing, 105
problems of practice groups, 130
professional boundaries, respecting, 81
professional development
    affinity, 128–129
    equity training, 113–117, 121–124
pulse meetings
    agenda template, 150
    guiding principles for effective pulse meetings, 143–144
    for information gathering, 56, 58–60, 60*f*
    sample topics and questions for pulse meetings, 145–147

race in schools, addressing vs. avoiding, 23–27
racial affinity groups. *See also* educators of color
    about, 125
    benefits of, 125–126, 128*f*
    communicating the purpose of, 133–134
    critiques and counterarguments, 131–132
    facilitators, identifying, 135
    goal of, 135
    leading for inclusion through, 132–136
    logistics and resources needed, 134–135
    planning for, 133
    political engagement and activism, 126–127
    purpose of, 131
    teacher voices on, 124, 136
    for white educators, 126–127, 131–132
racial affinity groups, forms of
    affinity professional development, 128–129
    identity-based mentoring, leadership, and advancement programs, 129–130
    leadership structures, 130
    problems of practice groups, 130
    regional groups, 129
    web-based communities, 129
racial justice, meaning of, 35–36
racial memory activity, 30
reflection, meaning of, 18
reflection and learning, fostering supportive environments for, 102–103
reflection and self-awareness, cultivating
    activities for, 30–31, 37
    necessity of, 19–23
    summary, 137–138
reflection and self-awareness, strategies for cultivating
    interrogate biases, 28–29
    intersectionality, 35–39
    ponder intent and impact, 31–35, 34*f*
reflection document, 61*f*
relationships, student–teacher, 7, 9
retention, 55, 111
role models, educators of color as, 8
root cause analysis, 62*f*

sample topics and questions for pulse meetings, 145–147
school instructional priorities, communicating, 77
School Readiness Tool, 52–54*f*

schools
    addressing vs. avoiding race in, 23–27
    culturally affirming, requirements for, 111
    foundational elements of, 43–46
    social roles, 6
school-to-prison pipeline, 7–8
segregation
    in schools, 24, 25f, 26f
    state-sanctioned, 131
self-awareness, elements of, 19
Social Identity Reflection Tool, 141–143
staff dynamics
    in a diverse workforce, 46–48
    readiness assessment, 53f
standardization, barrier to culturally responsive education, 97–98
stay interviews, 56
stereotypes, 75
students of color, percent of enrolled students, 1, 7
students with disabilities, 11
surveys, 56–58, 58f

teacher certification programs, 71–72
teachers. *See also* educators of color; educator workforce
    capacity and resources, fostering supportive environments for, 102–104
    planning and collaboration, prioritizing, 103–104
    planning time, minimizing interferences to, 81
    relationships, student–teacher, 7, 9

vision and mission statements, 43–44, 52f

well-being, educator, 81–82
white students
    educator diversity, benefits to, 8–9
    percent of enrolled students, 6–7
white teachers
    racial affinity groups, 126–127, 131–132
    turnover statistics, 14f
white women teachers, percent of workforce, 1, 12

About the Author

Andrea Terrero Gabbadon, PhD, is a professor of education, professional learning designer and facilitator, and qualitative researcher based in Philadelphia, Pennsylvania. Andrea's work explores the relationshipbetween school organizational conditions, educator diversity, and culturally responsive and sustaining practices and systems. Founder and principal consultant at ILM Consulting Group, Andrea interacts with both preservice and current education practitioners through invited presentations, workshops at state and national conferences, teacher coaching, and professional learning facilitation. Her work with ILM has also supported the design and launch of several innovative schools serving ethno-racially diverse students in urban areas.

As an educator affiliated with institutions of higher education such as Temple University and Swarthmore College, Andrea has taught undergraduate and graduate courses in education. She has mentored school leaders and K–12 teachers on research-based best practices and culturally responsive approaches. A former high school teacher in traditional public and charter schools, Andrea also has a background in instructional leadership, having served as a director of curriculum and instruction and administrator of a turnaround high school. Andrea earned a bachelor's degree in secondary education and Spanish at Temple University, a master's degree in school leadership from the University of Pennsylvania, and a doctorate in policy and organizational studies from Temple University.

Related ASCD Resources

At the time of publication, the following resources were available (ASCD stock numbers in parentheses):

Becoming a Globally Competent School Leader by Ariel Tichnor-Wagner (#119011)

Cultural Competence Now: 56 Exercises to Help Educators Understand and Challenge Bias, Racism, and Privilege by Vernita Mayfield (#118043)

Culture, Class, and Race: Constructive Conversations That Unite and Energize Your School Community by Brenda CampbellJones, Shannon Keeny, and Franklin CampbellJones (#118010)

Five Practices for Equity-Focused School Leadership by Sharon I. Radd, Gretchen Givens Generett, Mark Anthony Gooden, and George Theoharis (#120008)

Fix Injustice, Not Kids: And Other Principles for Transformative Equity Leadership by Paul Gorski and Katy Swalwell (#120012)

Leading Within Systems of Inequity in Education: A Liberation Guide for Leaders of Color by Mary Rice-Boothe (#123014)

Leading Your School Toward Equity: A Practical Framework for Walking the Talk by Dwayne Chism (#123003)

Stay and Prevail by Nancy Gutiérrez and Roberto Padilla (#123006)

For up-to-date information about ASCD resources, go to www.ascd.org. You can search the complete archives of *Educational Leadership* at www.ascd.org/el. To contact us, send an email to member@ascd.org or call 1-800-933-2723 or 703-578-9600.

WHOLE CHILD
TENETS

HEALTHY
Each student enters school healthy and learns about and practices a healthy lifestyle.

SAFE
Each student learns in an environment that is physically and emotionally safe for students and adults.

ENGAGED
Each student is actively engaged in learning and is connected to the school and broader community.

SUPPORTED
Each student has access to personalized learning and is supported by qualified, caring adults.

CHALLENGED
Each student is challenged academically and prepared for success in college or further study and for employment and participation in a global environment.

The ASCD Whole Child approach is an effort to transition from a focus on narrowly defined academic achievement to one that promotes the long-term development and success of all children. Through this approach, ASCD supports educators, families, community members, and policymakers as they move from a vision about educating the whole child to sustainable, collaborative actions.

Support and Retain Educators of Color relates to the **safe, engaged,** and **supported** tenets.

For more about the ASCD Whole Child approach, visit **www.ascd.org/wholechild.**

Become an ASCD member today!
Go to www.ascd.org/joinascd
or call toll-free: 800-933-ASCD (2723)

DON'T MISS A SINGLE ISSUE OF ASCD'S AWARD-WINNING MAGAZINE.

ascd educational leadership

If you belong to a Professional Learning Community, you may be looking for a way to get your fellow educators' minds around a complex topic. Why not delve into a relevant theme issue of *Educational Leadership*, the journal written by educators for educators?

Subscribe now, or purchase back issues of ASCD's flagship publication at **www.ascd.org/el**. Discounts on bulk purchases are available.

To see more details about these and other popular issues of *Educational Leadership*, visit **www.ascd.org/el/all**.

ascd

2800 Shirlington Road
Suite 1001
Arlington, VA 22206 USA

www.ascd.org/learnmore

www.ingramcontent.com/pod-product-compliance
Lightning Source LLC
Chambersburg PA
CBHW070559010526
44118CB00012B/1388